The Chapters of my Life

By

Phil Brock

The Chapters of my Life

By

Phil Brock

ISBN: 978-0-9927664-0-5

This book is published by Phil Brock in conjunction with **WRITERSWORLD**, and is produced entirely in the UK. It is available to order from most bookshops in the United Kingdom, and is also globally available via UK based Internet book retailers.

Copy edited by Ian Large
Cover design by Jag Lall

WRITERSWORLD
2 Bear Close Flats, Bear Close, Woodstock
Oxfordshire, OX20 1JX, England
☎ 01993 812500
☎ +44 1993 812500

www.writersworld.co.uk

The text pages of this book are produced via an independent certification process that ensures the trees from which the paper is produced come from well managed sources that exclude the risk of using illegally logged timber while leaving options to use post-consumer recycled paper as well.

To Brenda,
for sharing and caring.

THE CHAPTERS OF MY LIFE

CHAPTER 1
My Life During The War

Life changed dramatically for me at the age of seven years and five days. In August 1939, we went to Scarborough for our usual fortnight's summer holiday and at that age I had no idea what was in store for me. Gran had lived with us from the time I was six months old, but my grandfather had died a few years earlier, under really tragic circumstances.

My mother's parents had gone on a late holiday and, in the rush to pack, my grandfather had forgotten his shaving brush. He bought a cheap one from the chemist, and whilst shaving one morning he cut himself slightly but thought no more about it at the time. Later he became ill, and apparently the bristles of the shaving brush had harboured anthrax. He died within ten days, since in those days there was no cure, and apparently his last days were absolute agony.

About three weeks before he died, my mother-to-be went to a fair with some of her friends where they all had their fortunes told. There was much laughing and giggling when it came to her turn, because the fortune teller indicated that she would rather not give any report. The general question was, "What is going to happen in Doris's life that was not to be mentioned?" It seems my mother pressed the fortune teller to give her a forecast, and the whole mood of the visit changed. She was told that she was going to lose a member of the family very shortly and that it would be someone very close to her. The fortune teller seemed genuinely sorry when telling her this. It was about three weeks later that her parents went on that fateful holiday, where the prediction sadly came true...

So now, in 1939, our household consisted of Mum, Dad, Gran and me. The significance of seven years and five days was the date on the calendar – the third of September 1939 – when, at 11am, Neville Chamberlain made his fateful speech. Britain was at war with Germany and this was the first day of the Second World War. I imagine that most youngsters of my age knew little of the world situation and I most certainly didn't! My father was quite a serious man so he must have read a great deal about the carnage of the First World War. He was well aware that he would be 'called up', and was determined that we were not going to spend the war in a major city where the bombing was likely to be considerable.

None of this was conveyed to me. Up to that point, I'd had a fairly sheltered upbringing. For example, the abdication of the King in 1937 was talked about in hushed tones, and I really didn't know why it had to happen.

Many other children were taken with their schools from the larger cities into the country en masse, but my father was determined that after he was called up, the rest of our little family would stay together. And so it was that we drove away from Hull with three large suitcases, to the little town of Market Weighton, about twenty miles from Hull, where at the time we knew no one. I have no idea how the contact was made, but we pulled up at Layton's Joiners and Undertakers, and before nightfall we were installed in the first of three cottages which was linked by a single door to the main house. Kath, the daughter of the family, who later became more like Auntie Kath to me, was away for the weekend in the Lake District with her friend, Winnie. As they returned by train in the evening, the lights at Selby Station had all been extinguished and they thought there had just been a power cut. The first Kath knew that war had been declared was when she arrived back home to learn that three complete strangers were asleep in what had been her part of the house. The prevailing mood at the time was, "It'll all be over by Christmas."

My father went back home and visited us at weekends. When, within a few months, he had to join the army, our house in Hull was boarded up to remain empty until the war ended. Here in Market Weighton, everything was new and different for me, and since the cottage was linked to the main house, we lived together as a family, with the Laytons. Little did we know that this was the start of a life-long friendship for all involved!

* * * * * * * * * * * * * * * * * * *

I don't imagine many people remember much from their very early childhood, but apparently my mother had a very difficult home birth. At one point, Dr Morton Stewart came downstairs to tell my father that he could save my mother, but not the baby. However, after his return upstairs, there was a wailing and it appeared that I had made it! This accounts for the fact that my middle name is Morton.

Later, I can remember having my tonsils and adenoids removed in hospital, but my next hospital visit was when I had to have a mastoid operation, which in those days was very serious indeed. This must have been when I was about five years old, but there have been no long-term problems. I was friendly with Christopher Clegg and his younger sister, Mary, and David Kelsey, who later made quite a name for himself in the theatre. The Clegg family came to Market Weighton for a few weeks in the early part of the war, but after that we lost touch with them all.

Friends from Market Weighton, c. 1942.

Another story from my earlier years happened when I was four or five years old on a visit to my paternal grandparents. We were in their garden in September. They had an apple tree which had never borne fruit, and my grandfather said, "If anyone can see an apple on that tree, I will give them a penny!" Little Mr Clever Dick claimed he could see one. It was a big tree and the one I claimed to be able to see was right at the top. The whole situation could have been defused if one of the adults had laughed and told me to stop being silly, but the atmosphere became quite tense, and I stuck with my story and got the penny. As we walked home, I could feel the penny in my pocket and I knew that I had lied. My parents also knew, and I knew they knew, and we walked home in complete silence. Nothing else was ever mentioned but I felt really ashamed, and I vowed there and then in my mind that I would NEVER AGAIN tell a lie. That early memory has stuck with me, so perhaps the incident served some purpose.

* * * * * * * * * * * * * * * * * * * *

Mr Walker Layton was the owner of the joinery and undertaking company, but by the time we arrived he was lying really ill and his eldest son, William, had taken over. Walker Layton had been responsible for starting the town band years before and, one Sunday morning, all the players formed a circle outside the room where he was lying so ill and played a selection of their repertoire for about twenty minutes. Many of them would be called up, and it was as if they were saying a final goodbye to him. Even though I was so young, I remember feeling really sad about it all.

Although I didn't know it at the time, the man of the house had cancer, and within a very short time, sadly, he died. My new family then consisted of his wife and daughter who were like another gran and auntie for me, plus my gran, mother and me. I have always been surprised at how adaptable children are to changed circumstances, and I adapted really well to life in the country.

We all had breakfast and dinner together in the main kitchen but at teatime, gran, mother and me had tea in the cottage, just the three of us. After I had gone to bed, the rest all had supper together. How the finances and the rations were sorted out, I never knew, but we paid ten shillings a week rent for the cottage. We had many advantages compared with the tenants of the other two cottages, where they paid only three and sixpence (about seventeen and a half pence) a week rent! I spent almost every night of the war on a camp bed but never had problems sleeping. The earth toilet was along the path down the garden, bathing was once a week in a wooden tub in front of the fire, and there was no hot water system in the house. I went up to bed by the light of a candle because electric lighting was only downstairs, the cooking was done on the kitchen range – and I loved it all!

Shortages were soon in full swing and everyone had a ration book with 'points' for nearly everything. These were actually issued from October 1939, but not brought into use until early the following year. At one stage, the lard ration went down to one ounce each per week, and the sugar ration was eight ounces per person. When I became convinced that I was not getting my share of sugar, Mother weighed it out for me in my own basin. By Tuesday of the following week I had used it all, and it came home to me that certain sacrifices were being made to my advantage. I never complained again.

Although the general feeling was that the war would not last for long, arrangements were made for me to go to the infant school. The teacher there was Miss Stevenson, who I remember as being elderly and very kind. The one-room school had no central heating, but an open fire with a guard in front. On very cold mornings, we trooped round the room for a few minutes, so that each of us could be near the fire for a short time. I can't remember being cold at all, but it provided a diversion from school work!

When I went to the 'big' school, where there were nearly a hundred pupils, I was the only boy who wore shoes; all the others wore boots. I can remember pleading with my mother to buy me a pair of boots. Looking back on those stringent times, I suppose my shoes had to be 'worn out' before new footwear could be bought.

The headmaster was Mr Cullingford, who had been shell-shocked in the First World War. As a result, he made involuntary movements all the time, and when he administered the cane, which was done quite routinely and regularly, it could land anywhere between halfway up the arm and the fingertips! I cannot remember ever seeing him smile, and he exercised the cane with tremendous gusto. There were three classes and initially I had Miss Mendham as my form teacher. My main memory of her was that she 'read' stories from the Old Testament, but using her own words so that the lesson was really story time. She was brilliant and succeeded in bringing the Old Testament history to life for us.

Back at my new home, the resident family had a cat which was known simply as 'Awd Cat'. Almost the first happy event for me was that Awd Cat had four kittens in my mother's hat box. I was totally fascinated; she must have had a friend on her nocturnal wanderings, because on average she produced about two litters a year! From that first litter, only one kitten was kept. We called it Sooty – not very original since it was black. Later, one more was kept from a further litter; this was Tiddles. Tiddles spent increasing lengths of time at a house just down the road and finally deserted us altogether.

Most of life was very basic, but there was a huge electric washing machine which was kept in the garage. Every Monday morning it was trundled along the path into the kitchen. It was really magnificent, much more than twice the size of a modern washing machine, and very powerful. One day during the holidays, I caught my right-hand middle finger in the wringer at the top. More by good luck than anything else, I reacted really quickly and reversed the rollers with my other hand which squeezed my finger out again. If I hadn't acted so quickly, I feel sure that I would have been seriously maimed.

Wednesday was baking day, and every week, 'Granny' Layton produced marvellous bread in the oven on the left of the kitchen range. She always said that she really enjoyed making bread, because it made her hands so white and clean!

At the end of the garden was an old hut where Amos lived. I never knew his second name. He looked and lived like a tramp, and in all honesty I was a bit afraid of him. Very shortly after we arrived at Market Weighton, he died. A little lad keeping in the background and 'ear wigging' can learn a lot about what goes on. The local doctor carried out a post mortem on the floor of the garage, and it seemed that he had died of natural causes.

Under his bed they found twenty-seven bibles, but apart from that, he had very few possessions. A coffin was made for him in the joiners' shop, but I have no idea who paid for it. When the sides of the coffin were being shaped, ten or twelve parallel saw cuts were made and the wood was carefully bent to a coffin shape. One of the saw cuts was made too deeply right through the wood for about four inches, and the gap had to be masked with wood filler. Someone said, "Well it's only for old Amos." Even as a seven-year-old I felt very sad and resentful that a human being could command such little respect.

The joiners' workshop was down the yard, and I spent many hours watching, listening and learning. I remember Ernie Dove very well and established a great friendship with him. He had two small children of his own and I learnt much from watching him in action. One day, when I was about ten, Ernie found our little cache of cigarettes and matches hidden in the old chicken shed. For a fortnight nothing was said and I suffered agonies, because I knew he must have found them. Finally, he brought out the little box and said, "What's all this then?" Although he knew my mother really well, he never told her. This impressed me greatly, but it cured us of that phase!

One Sunday at a place quite near to us, they slaughtered a pig. This was against the law! The police found out and descended on the crime scene, but by the time they arrived, the pig had been butchered, shared out and the place was cleaned up, so no evidence of the killing remained. But we lads knew all about it (ear wigging) and the small ditch running between two gardens was red with blood. I felt that the police had not been ALL that thorough in their search.

My introduction to bad language came when watching work in the joiners' shop. Various words were being used which were new to me, and one in particular seemed really strong. We were having tea in the cottage and the nights were drawing in, when I jumped up and said, "Let's have the bloody lights on." There was a shocked silence broken by my mother saying in a horrified tone, "WHERE did you hear THAT word?" My answer came over very shakily, "In the joiners' shop." The reply was most forceful, "Well YOU don't use that word!" I didn't really know that what I had said was wrong, but I was to learn quite quickly that there were a few other words that were not acceptable!

One day, two army officers arrived at the house and Mrs Layton was questioned about the possibility of having a couple of soldiers billeted on her. She was explaining to them that room could not possibly be made available for anyone else since, in addition to the two other cottages being occupied, a family from Hull was living in the first cottage. Little Mr Nosey Parker was ear wigging and piped up with, "What about the room where Mr Layton had been?"

I was really keen to have soldiers billeted with us. As a direct result of my intervention two soldiers were indeed installed. One outcome was that 'Auntie' Kath became very friendly with Raymond, and after the soldiers moved on, he and Kath kept in touch with each other. When the war was over, Kath and Raymond were married – we were invited to the wedding – and Raymond worked with the family firm for the rest of his life. They had a son, David, but if I had not spoken up when the billeting officers arrived, they would probably never even have met!

The fact that we were living with The Laytons helped greatly, as we were quickly accepted into the general community. For me in particular, it was important to be accepted at school. Some of the boys thought that we were really related to our host family and that Mrs Layton was actually my other gran. The Layton family had been living in the town for many years and there was a great deal of contact as a result of the business. The family were keen members of All Saints Church and were known for miles around. Quite a number of children were evacuated for a short time, but we were never regarded as evacuees. Later in the war, when families in Hull were bombed out and brought to the town temporarily, the locals talked quite openly in front of us, and in a critical way, about 'The people from Hull'. We were completely integrated!

The local cinema stayed open during the war and I went with other friends of my age to the Saturday afternoon matinee, which was almost always a cowboy film. Three miles from the town was St. Williams, a reformatory school where boys were sent who had been in trouble with the police. Their age range seemed to be from about fourteen to seventeen, and on Saturday afternoons they were allowed to walk to Market Weighton to see the film. They wore khaki shirts and shorts, and I can never remember them being involved with any trouble. They appeared to be unsupervised and visited the local shops, but I imagine that the punishment for bad behaviour would have been that the privilege was removed for the following Saturday. Indeed they seemed to blend in really well and were friendly with my mates and me even though we were very much younger.

When I was about eight years old I was taken to Beverley for an appointment with the dentist, Alexander Smith. It seems that my teeth were crowding each other and were becoming very irregular. The dentist looked into my mouth and exclaimed with great feeling, "My God, what a mess!" I thought that his chair-side manner left much to be desired, particularly when dealing with a youngster who was slumped down in the chair feeling absolutely petrified! He then went on to outline the various possibilities for treatment, each one sounding more terrifying than the previous one. Ever since that day I have been afraid of dentists, although now I am slightly more relaxed about this.

After discussion with my mother, he removed eight teeth, and the bleeding continued on the bus all the way home. A year or so later, I flew over the front handlebars of a friend's bike, and broke one of my two middle front teeth. Much later, I had it capped, but I was never very good at football because I used to hang back in case it was knocked out again. This actually happened twice during my teenage years and having it fixed back without anaesthetic was agony!

The local coach and haulage firm, R. and J. France, was just along the road from where we lived and the main house there had been the home of 'giant' John

Bradley who lived in the eighteen hundreds. For many years he was in the *Guinness Book of Records*, being nearly eight feet tall. All the doors in the house had been eight feet high, and after he died, the top part was filled with a window so the replacement doors could be of normal height.

One of the employees there worked in the office in the morning and in the garage in the afternoon. After he was called up to the forces, my mother secured the office work involved with his job, although she was not keen to take over the afternoons! She gave great satisfaction and later, when the family decided to have a holiday, we were asked to stay for a week to look after the place. The house was an absolute warren of rooms with all sorts of equipment (junk!), and I was in my element. At the end of the week though, I was very happy to return to our cottage at the Laytons, even though I had enjoyed the change.

Regular dances were held at the Church Hall and Kath and my mother used to go along quite regularly. One evening, 'our' two soldiers decided to go along the road, hide in the shadows and then surprise them on their way home. The plan rather backfired, since when they realised that they were being followed, Kath and my mother started to hurry and then to run. In front of the house next door to us was a boot scraper; my mother tripped over it and must have landed very heavily indeed. The first I knew about this was on the following morning when Mother had a black eye and much bruising. However, neither she nor Kath held it against them, and, indeed, one of the soldiers was Raymond who Kath later married!

The Christmases I had at Market Weighton were some of the best I can remember; seen through my young eyes they were magical. Before our second Christmas there, Mother said, "Things are a bit tight at present. I don't think Father Christmas will be able to come up with much this year." Like a fool, I said, "We'll have to see what Mother Christmas will be able to manage." The cat was out of the bag, but the fun of it all was kept going throughout my childhood.

Although Christmas was so exciting for me I never paused to wonder how much the adults were enjoying it all. My father had been posted to Aden, where he stayed for the entire war with a signals unit. My mother and father had different temperaments, but they were very close indeed as I realised much more when I was older. Kath was without Raymond, who was abroad, Mrs Layton had lost her husband so recently, and Gran had been without her husband for many years, but they all made it a happy time, largely to make it a happy time for me, I suppose.

After Walker Layton had died, Granny Layton seldom went out at all, apart from going down the yard to the joiners' workshop. When a coffin had been made there, she would come back up to the house and urge my gran to go down to see it, but I don't think the invitation was ever acted upon.

However, after tea on Christmas Day, we all went up the town to Southgate, to spend the evening with Kath's brother, Les and his wife Norah and their daughter, Maisie. She and I saw quite a bit of each other because she used to visit her gran quite regularly, and when Les was on duty with the Observer Corps down Sweep Lane, we used to go down to visit him. On Christmas Day evening, when Les returned from the British Legion, we played banker for pennies, and I particularly enjoyed that part of the evening. We used to leave there at about two o'clock in the morning and have a good 'lie in' on the same day.

Another aspect of life which added to the fun was the 'wireless' (radio). The artists I particularly remember were George Formby with his ukulele, Jewel and Warriss, Sandy Powell ("Can you hear me Mother?"), and Rob Wilton ("The day war broke out"). However, the one programme which I remember more than all the others was *It's That Man Again* (ITMA) – Tommy Handley. The catchphrases seemed never-ending and Tommy Handley himself was a national treasure, keeping everyone laughing right through the war. Every Thursday evening at 8.30pm, I sat close to the wireless sitting on the back of one of the chairs while the adults played cards. However, comedy is forever changing, and when some repeats of the show were broadcast thirty years later, I wondered why we had all laughed so much!

There was a piggery building down the yard and the pigs were owned by a consortium which included my mother. She used to take turns at 'mucking out' and feeding them. Granny Layton kept chickens and sometimes ducks and later on we had some geese – three, I think. I kept rabbits, a buck and a doe, and mated them from time to time. Relating to this, Mother said, "You mustn't watch them you know", but when I asked why, the reply was not really convincing. We boys used to put the two rabbits together in the old chicken run, and then sit on the roof of our den to cheer them on! While I was there, we made several dens, each successive one being better than the one before.

Mentioning our dens reminds me of what freedom we enjoyed. We used to roam all over the countryside without anyone worrying about us. In my friend Brian's yard, we made a small pond and concreted it out. No one had given permission; we just did it. On seeing it in the early stages, Brian's father was greatly amused and said it looked like the start of a grave being dug, but there was no suggestion that we shouldn't have done it, nor that we should have asked first.

In the same yard, many of the buildings were quite old, and there was a gap of about six inches between the back of one building and the much higher Co-op building next door. One Saturday morning, we heard scratching and when we climbed on the low roof, we found that a chicken had slipped right to the bottom and was trapped. We tried to induce it to go up a narrow plank which we had pushed in at an angle, but the bird must have thought that we were trying to kill it! Without reference to anyone, we smashed a hole in the wall near the floor (only single brick thickness), big enough for the chicken to escape, which it did like lightning. We repaired the wall and reported the incident afterwards, but we said nothing beforehand in case the move had been forbidden. Again, no punishment followed, but we simply knew it was the right thing to do.

Just to the north of the town was a field of several acres which was common land. This was known as the Monkey Run, as it still is today. I have no idea how it came to be called that, but we were very familiar with it and used to play there quite often. The greater part of it sloped gently to the east, and the slope increased being finally bordered by a stream. We played all sorts of games there including splashing in the stream in summer. One day we met up with a boy who attended a private school. I had always thought he was rather 'posh', but that evening he joined the four of us and just fitted in with what we were doing. We discovered he was much the same as us, which was a valuable lesson!

Very shortly after the war started, the ice cream van visited for the last time. None of us tasted ice cream again until the war ended. Milk was supplied in two cans carried round by Millie (we never knew her other name). When milk was delivered to a house, the resident had to produce a jug and the milk was ladled into it. Millie seemed to be delivering from morning until night. When we saw her in the evening after we had just bought our 'pennyworth of chips', she would accept a chip from each of us. We couldn't afford fish very often; a fish cost four pence (the equivalent of about two pence in today's money).

Brian Wilson and I were particularly good friends, and on one occasion he found a mortar bomb. Of course, he brought it up the garden and we all gathered to look at it and poke it. We ALL forgot the advice which had been drummed into us not to touch anything which looked suspicious, and I think we were quite disappointed when it turned out to be a dummy. If it had been real however...

Brian's grandma had a pub along the main street, and she had remarried a man who we knew as 'Old Ranji'. We had never met him, and he was really scruffy, but one evening, three of us were trying to climb the lamp post just outside Layton's yard. When we saw him approaching, we pretended to be just talking to each other. As he came along, he said gruffly, "Isn't even one of you going to climb it?" We started trying again and with his encouragement, we all made it to the top. We found that he was quite friendly, which even surprised Brian!

The far end of Layton's property was known as 'down t'garth', and at the very bottom there was a neglected patch. This was yet another area where we could really do as we liked. Years before, two large ash trees had been cut down and several smaller trees had grown from round each of the stumps. The diameter of these varied from about two inches to four inches and one day we decided to cut these down. Here again, we didn't consider it necessary to ask permission, because nobody else ever went down there. We ended up with about a dozen really long poles. These we cut into lengths and made a frame for yet another den. When we had finished weaving together straw and long grass, it ended up fairly rainproof, although we did not put this to the test when it was actually raining. We were very proud of our efforts.

At the other side of the property was a huge elm tree. I remember the time when we were old enough and strong enough to climb it, and we made a stout platform about fifteen feet from the ground. When we climbed further, we could see over the top of the joiners' workshop to the houses beyond. Many of the neighbours' gardens were within viewing distance of the tree and I'm afraid we enjoyed acting dangerously up there, basically to show off.

There was no scout group in the town, as it had been disbanded during the war, due to lack of leaders, but a new vicar was appointed for the Parish Church. The Rev. J.M. Mundy was a qualified scout leader and when he started the scout troop, which covered boys from eleven to fifteen years of age, I was keen to join. I had always wanted to be involved with scouting and when the first batch of older boys had been admitted, I was with the next batch.

However, I began to understand that all this could not last, because the war was coming to an end. I had gone to Market Weighton as a seven-year old, a child, but by the time we moved back home, I was nearly a teenager. The comparative freedom ended for me, and I had to settle down to life in Hull. I always remember that point as being the end of my childhood, but after returning to Hull, I quickly 'joined up' again in the Portobello (Methodist) Scout Group. This has been a very big part of my life, and later there is a chapter about my involvement.

What amazes me about the years I spent at Market Weighton is that although we knew nothing whatsoever about the Layton family before the day war broke out, we lived together as a family for over five years and really did forge relationships which lasted a lifetime. In those early years, 'Granny' Layton and Kath were like another granny and auntie to me. After the war, I visited them regularly, particularly in the run-up to Christmas. Kath once said to me that it didn't seem like Christmas was coming until they had a visit from me, often accompanied by my mother. Much later, Kath and Raymond even drove to my father's funeral at Scarborough, despite the fact that they were well past middle age themselves.

It has only been very recently that I realised how very lucky we were. A friend of mine, who left Hull in his pram, and came to Market Weighton with his older brother and mother, told me that they hadn't enjoyed it, because where they were living, they didn't feel at all welcome. They only stayed for a short time and then moved on. When we first arrived at the Laytons, we were complete strangers to them, but in no time at all, we were living like a real family!

Tailpiece: As a child, I had no proper understanding of what the war was all about, and for me, our move to Market Weighton was a great adventure. I was not really concerned about my father being away, since so many other things were different about my life. As news of the war filtered through to me by way of newsreels at the cinema and reports on the wireless, it all seemed so divorced from the life that I was enjoying. No one from my immediate family and friends was killed, or even injured, and I was only aware of the world situation in a very vague way. It was much later, when I was older, that the tragedy and suffering involved was really brought home to me. Immediately after the war ended, two things puzzled me as a young teenager. During the war, the Russians had been our allies, and had been on 'our side'. After the war ended they were suddenly our enemies! The change seemed to be quite sudden, and although relationships have improved over the years, there still seems to be uneasiness in that area. The second thing was regarding Winston Churchill. During the war, when he broadcast to the nation, everyone went straight home to hear his every word. The following day, everyone was talking about what he had said, and it seemed to me that he was much loved – even revered. Yet following the first general election after the war, he was voted out of office!

CHAPTER 2
Going Back Home Again

When I was due to sit my eleven plus examination, I knew we would be going back home at the end of the war, so I sat for the Hull Authority examination and passed. This would enable me to go on to Malet Lambert High School in Hull. When the war continued, we stayed at Market Weighton for another year, so at the end of that academic year when the war still hadn't ended, I sat the examination for Beverley Grammar School and passed. Travelling by train to Beverley was awful for two main reasons. On reaching Beverley in the morning, I was faced with a twenty-minute walk in all weathers. In the afternoon, I had to leave school ten minutes before lessons ended in order to catch the return train, and whoever was teaching us for the last lesson was often irritated by this. Few youngsters would want to be different from the rest of the class in that way.

After two and a half terms at Beverley Grammar School, the war had ended and we moved back to Hull and from then I attended Malet Lambert High School, to be placed in the second year 'Remove' stream, which was for pupils who had failed their first attempt at the scholarship examination. As I had stayed an extra year in the school in Market Weighton, I had missed a year in the upper school, so I passed through the Remove form for my second and third year. If I had continued into the fifth year Remove, I would only have been able to take the School Certificate after a further two years. However, at that time, there was another stream of 'late developers' who had moved to the high school in their third year, and this was called 3X. They were allowed to take their school certificate at the end of their year five, and three of us were switched from the Remove into this form. I feel that someone in the hierarchy had a sense of humour because it was then known as Five Omega!

Our Form Master was Mr Grewe, who had only recently arrived on the staff. He was totally brilliant and eventually became the headmaster. He was an excellent teacher, a really hard worker and I felt he took an interest in every one of us. My results in the School Certificate Examination were such that I was able to pass into the sixth form for a further two years, and at that stage I had made up my mind that I wanted to be a teacher. The incentive for working hard was that if you didn't, you would be expelled! Academically, I always regarded myself as fairly average; I was not a natural scholar but good with practical problems. Some of the teachers were inspiring, others were very strict indeed, some were downright unpleasant, and some treated pupils in a very detached way with very little rapport.

Shortly after we moved back to Hull, my father was demobilised from the army but I regarded this with apprehension rather than excitement. It was not entirely his fault, although I can never remember us having much to say to each other after the war. He had been away for over five years and we had lost touch with each other. I was never a very wayward child but I did get into mischief from time to time, and the mantra was always the same: "You wait until your father gets home; he'll sort you out!" This wasn't really fair to him.

I began to wonder if I really wanted him to come back at all. He always seemed to be ill at ease with me and, looking back, I feel he didn't really understand what our relationship should be. I believe his father had been very strict with him and because of this he had no real role model to follow. He had many friends, was a popular person in company, and he and my mother were absolutely devoted to each other. I was always well cared for, we had nice holidays, he never laid hands on me, but he always seemed distant. I could never imagine us going out to have a drink together, or for the two of us just to socialise in any way. When I had achieved anything, my mother would say, "Your father's ever so pleased with you, you know", and I would say, "Well, why can't HE tell me?" But he never did.

There was just one 'fun' situation which I remember with my father, and this was when he stayed at Laytons for Christmas 1939, just before he had to join the army. On Christmas morning, he banned all the adults from our part of the house and produced coloured paper, string and glue. We cut all sorts of garments from the coloured paper and glued each one to a long length of string, so that when it was held up it looked like a washing line.

With reference to the war, there was a heavy line of defences made somewhere on the continent supposedly to stop the advance of the German army taking over other countries, and this was known as the Siegfried Line. The comedy song of the time was, "We're going to hang out the washing on the Siegfried Line. Have you any dirty washing mother dear?" (I can imagine some of the older readers singing it now!) When the washing line was ready, he took hold of one end of the string and I held the other end, and we opened the connecting door holding it aloft and singing the song. After we had paraded it round the kitchen, it was fastened aloft to add to the decorations which were already in place.

* * * * * * * * * * * * * * * * * *

For most of my early life we had a really good family friend. He was Gran's 'boyfriend', although he must have been middle-aged even before the war. He was Irish – Michael O'Connell – and he was a real fun person, always cheerful and with a wealth of stories, which over the years I heard time and time again. Long before that, he had been retired from the Irish Constabulary, and I never knew until after he died that one of his three medals which he left to me, was for bravery in saving someone from drowning, although he himself was a non-swimmer.

Before the war, he would visit us every day and he was always ready for a game and a laugh. In addition, he was always coming up with snatches of songs which caused a great deal of amusement. My gran was called Annie, but he always called her, 'Gertie'. The family called him 'O.C.' and I shall never know why, but I called him 'Coke'. The strange thing was that in a very short time, all the family were calling him 'Coke'. I wish I'd been encouraged to call him 'Grandad', because that was what he really was for me. During the war, he lived in Hull, and as he had a key, he visited our house regularly to check the property. On examining all our furniture and possessions when we returned to Hull, I found that he had labelled everything with our name and address, in case the house had suffered from enemy action. It must have taken him hours.

Later on, he dropped the 'O' and became Michael Connell, so that people wouldn't know he was from Ireland. This was in spite of the fact that he had a marvellous accent as broad as the Irish Sea. He came to see us every two or three weeks when we were at Market Weighton and after the war, when he came to see us, he and I used to have a game of bowls in East Park. We were about the same standard and I'm sure he didn't go easy on me. He had a smart upright gait, always carried an umbrella and always wore a suit with waistcoat and tie. He never stayed the night and in the evening, he and Gran would go for a drink in the town and then she would see him off on the train.

Before the war, one of the national newspapers, the *News Chronicle*, ran a competition in the summer, in an effort to increase its circulation. A character called 'Lobby Lud' would be at a different seaside town every day and the location for each day was published every week. This man had to be challenged by a holidaymaker who carried the morning paper and the challenge was – "You are Lobby Lud of the *News Chronicle* and I claim my five pounds." Coke always wore a suit, even on the beach and he always carried a rolled umbrella. When he was with us on holiday in Scarborough, he used to be challenged time and again on the day that Lobby Lud was there, and of course he had to deny it, but with great good humour and laughter all round.

O.C., my grandma and my father at Scarborough, 1937.

Scarborough has always been very special for me, because I was only eleven months old when the family stayed at Aunty Mary's for the first time. This was a boarding house on the north side, overlooking the bay and it was then called

Beeley House. We stayed there every year for seven years, until war was declared. Mary always related well to the children and, after the war, we stayed there for a fortnight every year, until I was a mid-teenager. Coke came to Scarborough with us right up to the war starting, but by the end of the war, he was living in West Yorkshire. He still came to see us every three or four weeks, but didn't come to Scarborough with us.

'Auntie' Mary – where we always stayed at Scarborough.

Much later, when he had turned ninety and was in hospital in Leeds, I went to see him one Saturday and took him a bottle of whisky – his favourite drink. All the sparkle seemed to have left him. My parents were returning from holiday on the following Tuesday and he knew that they were going to visit him. After they returned home early on the Tuesday evening, mother rang me to say that they had found him looking really ill and, sadly, I was able to confirm that. Only half an hour later she rang me again to say that the hospital had been in touch, and he had died. Nothing will ever cause me to doubt that he had hung on to see them for one last time. He was ninety-two years old, but to me, he never seemed to have changed at all. He was smart and ramrod upright, almost to the end.

Sadly, Gran died before he did at seventy-nine. In her final years, her memory let her down badly and she would ask the same question again and again within the space of about ten minutes. Someone had to be with her at all times and one Saturday morning both my parents wanted to go out, so I was left in charge. Halfway through the morning, I remembered that I wanted to go out as well and asked if she would come with me. She readily agreed, got her fur coat on and I hoisted her into my van. I had three calls to make and parked outside each shop. (This was well before yellow lines decorated our roads!) She thoroughly enjoyed the trip, and each time I returned to the van, she cheerfully told me about what she had seen.

When my parents returned, I told them of our trip. "I haven't been anywhere", Gran said, sounding really grumpy. I led her into the front room and pointed to the van. Again, sounding really grumpy, she said, "I certainly haven't been out in THAT thing!" I gave up, but I knew she had enjoyed it at the time. The following Friday she woke up and told Mother she still felt tired. "Turn over and get a bit more sleep", said Mum, and when she went upstairs less than an hour later, Gran had died. Although it was sad at the time, several people remarked to me that they hoped they could end their lives in this way rather than lying on a bed of sickness or being in pain for ages and ages.

I remember the day when my father came home from work, on the day that he retired at sixty-two. His working life was over and I can remember feeling sad for him, even though he was delighted. After the war, his ambition had been to have a smallholding, and there had been many trips round the East Riding looking at possible properties. He never found anywhere suitable and I began to think that it had all been a 'pipe dream'.

However, after he retired, he and mum moved to Scarborough, where they had enjoyed so many happy times, and they always said that every single day was like a holiday. But he never realised his dream of having a smallholding and he hadn't liked working in an office, which he did for most of his working life. What he really did enjoy was photography, and he had several of his photographs published in the *Reckitts* magazine.

They had five years at Scarborough, and it was only later that I discovered they had been quite short of money. My father was too proud to draw the dole and my mother would not cash any of the small number of shares that she had been left by Gran.

* * * * * * * * * * * * * * * * * *

Referring back to my time as a pupil at school, I can remember very few occasions when I was spellbound or vitally interested in the work. I was not a natural scholar but the main motivation involved learning and working hard. This is no bad lesson in itself but with English Literature, for example, I was really bored by the way it was taught. Not until I was much older did I see a production of *Henry IV* at Stratford, and I sat there absolutely enthralled!

When I was made to take part during a play reading, I was quite nervous and read far too fast. Mrs Fawcett would address the class with the words, "Alright, Brock is showing off again", and pass the part to someone else. In truth, I was terrified! Mrs Fawcett was the producer for the plays presented by the Old Pupils Association, and they always maintained a very high standard. She was really brilliant, but I doubt that any pupil could ever say that she was even remotely friendly.

Mrs Earnshaw once gave me a real 'clattering' on the head. I can't remember what I had said or done, but I do remember that I had deserved it and was not at all resentful. Much later, she was appointed as Senior Mistress at East Mount, where I was Head of Science. Neither of us mentioned our previous encounter!

As a youngster, I normally never swore at all but on one occasion, a quite mild incident assumed a much bigger consequence for me. About halfway through a lesson, I had needed something from my desk and, in closing it, dropped the lid on one of my fingers. My very muted, "damn" – little more than a whisper – really brought damnation on me. Miss Hill went ballistic and sent me into the corridor, where I waited in fear and trembling, convinced that I was going to be expelled. At the end of the lesson, I was left there as the rest of the class filed out, and was again faced by Miss Hill who gave me another ear-bashing, expressing loathing and disgust regarding my outburst. I was so relieved that I would be returning to school on the following day that I took it like a man, although a rather shaken man!

Sport was never stressed to any great extent. The double period allocated to football in winter and cricket in summer was regarded as free time by the staff involved. There was no great rush to get started, and once the basic arrangements were made, the staff disappeared. I enjoyed PE and was quite good in the gym, and at one point when we were doing high jump, I was told that I was a natural scissor jumper. There was no suggestion of extra coaching and I was not really interested anyway. Mr Royle took a swimming group, but it was on Friday nights which clashed with the scout meeting, so – no contest there. Mr Magee ran the harvest camps during the summer holidays. I enjoyed the time spent on a farm, and the extra incentive was that we were paid!

In the sixth form we were usually treated much more like young adults although the thought of being expelled still filled me with concern. In the Upper Sixth, Mr Magee – 'Trigger', but not to his face – taught Pure Maths and Applied Maths, and he was a brilliant teacher. However, after about five weeks of our first term with him, he strode in and played absolute hell with us! We were lazy, not working, a complete waste of his time. Exercise books were thrown back to us, and at us, and all the time, we were harangued in a loud and forceful manner. Looking back, it just had to be an act on his part, but it seemed very real at the time! What made it worse was that the 'classroom' was a small room behind the stage, which would just contain the seven of us who were in the group. The whole performance lasted for the entire lesson, and from that point we really worked hard, at least for him.

However, quite some time after this interlude we learnt that he had a very human side. He always managed to end each period a few minutes before the bell, and would then say, "What are we going to talk about?" This happened on a regular basis and normally we were invited to give our opinion on the topic in hand. Thus it was that I finally realised that I had an opinion, and normally these discussions were very good humoured. However, when Ray Bewick floated the idea that Mr Magee would be much more popular in the lower school if he just 'let up' a bit, there was another explosion. "I'm not here to be popular! I'm here to do a job!", and much more in the same vein, so that we regretted the subject had been raised at all.

One topic raised was, "Can you remember the funniest film you've ever seen?" Mr Magee started telling us about a Charlie Chaplin film. He managed very well until Charlie was clattering down a staircase on a bed, and at some point in the dialogue, he started to break up. After trying really hard, he finally left the room almost crying. On two separate occasions, we returned to this, and asked if he could finish the story. Each time, he really tried, and each time he got a little bit further, but each time he finally left the room in a totally helpless state, and we never did hear the end of it.

Several years later, he and I met socially and he asked me to call him 'John'. Even though by that time, our relationship was totally friendly, I had just too much respect for him to call him by his first name. And at that stage, I didn't dare to ask him to finish the story of the Charlie Chaplin film. It might have killed him! He lived to be a good age and I met him and we talked on many occasions. I went to his funeral feeling very sad, but a friend of his spoke at the service saying that they had talked about a week before. Looking back on the conversation, he said that it was almost as if he was saying goodbye and apparently he died the same day. He was a good teacher and a good man, with a firm faith.

Tailpiece: During my schooldays, I found much of the work rather boring. The Scouts had become a big part of my life and I formed many friendships, which have lasted to the present day – over sixty years later. Life sometimes presents us with unusual challenges, and within three months of leaving school as a pupil, I was in the army.

CHAPTER 3
National Service

From the age of eighteen years all men were eligible for National Service in the army, the navy or the air force. The only exception was that a man who had started an apprenticeship could complete that first. All those who had been accepted for a teacher training college had to complete their National Service of two years BEFORE going to college. However, everyone had to pass a medical and if some health problem was discovered, he could be excused from service. I didn't particularly want to have my life disrupted, but I did want to pass the medical and emerge as A1. However, the mastoid operation on my right ear could have prevented me from being up to scratch. I attended the examination with trepidation and was referred to a specialist, but I emerged as totally fit – A1, in fact.

I opted to go into the army and within a few weeks I was called up and issued with a rail pass to York. Here, an army lorry was waiting for about twenty of us – all complete strangers to me – and we were transported to Strensall Camp to begin six weeks of basic training. In the first few days we were given aptitude tests and as a result of that, about thirty of us were transferred to the Officer Training Cadre. This involved ten weeks basic training instead of the usual six weeks, and we were divided into two squads, with a corporal in charge of each and an officer in overall charge.

Our NCO was Corporal Sullivan. I never regretted being allocated to his squad; he was suitably military when on parade, but was a very good instructor indeed and off parade was completely approachable. During the ten weeks, we went off in groups of five or six for a four-day session known as the War Office Selection Board or WOSB for short. Here, we each had various interviews and problem solving projects to assess whether we were commissioned officer material, but at this stage of my service, I was really not all that interested. About nine of our entire group qualified for officer training, but, not surprisingly, I failed! However, all of us completed the ten weeks basic training and after a further week of preparation, three went on to be lance corporals on the permanent staff at Strensall. I was one of them.

Corporal Sullivan was posted to a war zone and, within about a fortnight, news came through that he had been killed in action. I felt gutted on hearing this, not only because he had a wife and two young children, but because basically, he was a thoroughly decent man. I had grown to like him, and to respect him in a relatively short time, and he had paid the ultimate price for his service.

I was allocated to a platoon where the men had just started basic training. The instructors were a sergeant who sported an impressive row of medal ribbons and a fierce manner, a corporal who had the Military Medal, and me, who a few brief weeks earlier had been a mere civilian. One of the squad turned out to be someone whom I had known well, and we had played together as children, so this, too, was not really good for my morale. Finally, both the sergeant and the full corporal were involved elsewhere at the start of my first day so I was in charge of the platoon. It must have been obvious to the men that I myself was a 'rookie', and I was highly relieved when they both returned about half an hour later. Even aside from the bad start, I felt that for the first few months I was fairly useless.

After about four months as a drill and weapon training instructor, learning the hard way, I was called to the company office. I reported in, with a feeling of dread. It seemed that on the strength of putting camping down as one of my interests when I filled in a form within two or three days of joining the army, I was to be put in charge of the tentage on a Territorial Army camp, which was to be set up on Strensall Common. I moved my possessions to a bell tent about a mile away from the barracks, and with a squad of nine men began the task of pitching first bell tents and then marquees for the entire camp. I had never pitched a marquee in my life, but I am a quick learner (a great asset). The army manual regarding tentage stated that the manpower required for pitching a marquee was one NCO (non-commissioned officer) and thirty men. Had I been more experienced, I would have complained to the senior officer about my position, but as it was, we just got on with it, albeit slowly. Later, as the job was not being completed quickly enough, a sergeant from the main camp was called in with the required thirty men, to pitch the remaining marquees which were needed.

When the TA personnel started to arrive in fortnightly groups, several of us were allocated to demonstrate the guard mounting drill, so that there would be some continuity. There must have been about sixty or seventy on the permanent staff filling all the basic jobs so that the routine went smoothly. I well remember the man in charge of the mess tent, who was quite a character. Whenever he was due for some leave, he would always say, "I'm off home this weekend and when I go into the house, the second thing I do will be to take my hat off." His body language always left no one in any doubt regarding how he would first greet his wife!

Four of the 'tentage' squad, TA camp at Strensall. (Author second from left.)

There were about ten corporals and lance corporals, and each of us acted as guard commander every ten days along with three private soldiers. We mounted guard at 5pm and were on duty through the night until eight o'clock the following morning. The privates patrolled in turn doing two hours on and four hours off, but the guard commander had to remain alert the whole time. The duty officer could visit at any time, and a corporal friend of mine was put on a charge for merely having slipped his boots off at two o'clock in the morning! The guard room was a small marquee equipped with a telephone and not much else, and all permanent staff below the rank of sergeant had to be checked when leaving camp for an evening and on returning.

When I had previously been on guard in the main barracks, there were two NCOs and six men, and I was involved with booking personnel in and out. On their return, they were booked in, followed by the initials SPD. The first time I was involved with this, I imagined these were the initials of the corporal who was checking people in, so I entered my own initials PMB. When the guard commander that night looked at the book, he held it out to me and shouted, "What the hell is this?" Thus I discovered that SPD stood for, 'sober and properly dressed'! This was an assessment, not of me, but of each person reporting back to barracks.

Every morning on the TA camp, my little group toured the site checking to see if any tent pegs needed securing more firmly. The main pegs supporting the marquees were about three feet long and, as a rule, we gave each two or three blows with a mallet as we were checking round just to make sure that they were secure. One evening, I received a message about the marquee which was being used as a NAAFI tent. Apparently the ground was very wet indeed, and it seemed that the girls serving behind the counter were virtually paddling!

I checked all around the outside and discovered a mound of grass about six feet across and two feet high which had appeared since that morning. I pressed it at one side with my boot and the entire mound bounced gently up and down. The whole bulge was composed of water, which must have seeped sideways lifting the turf as it increased in volume. When we had checked the tent pegs that morning, the pointed end of one of the large pegs must have been just touching a water pipe, and by knocking it in slightly, we had caused a burst. This was reported immediately and the water had to be turned off until it was repaired.

I was on guard duty one night when about a dozen of the TA personnel arrived back in camp. They had their own guard room tent, but on this occasion, they had drifted slightly due to an over-enthusiastic intake of liquid refreshment (they were drunk!). As a young NCO, not yet nineteen, I would have been totally ineffective in defusing the situation, and so, staying in the shadows, I moved as near to them as possible. Using the deepest voice I could muster and speaking in as 'posh' a voice as I could, I shouted loudly, "You men over there! Get to your tents immediately or there will be trouble." An urgent voice shouted that it was the duty officer, and the rabble dispersed immediately!

After five weeks, without a free weekend, I applied for four days leave. Using my rail pass, I visited the Festival of Britain 1951, in London. Staying at the Union Jack Club was very economical, and during the four days, I visited the festival twice, saw three shows and toured the main landmarks of London which before I had only seen in pictures. The entire break cost less than five pounds and had all been entirely worthwhile. The most amusing incident was when a group of people, obviously Cockneys, were asking me to identify various landmarks along the Thames, and yet this was my first visit to the capital!

At the end of the camp when the last of the TA personnel had left, we were involved with clearing, and my most worrying experience was being in charge of the guard room during part of this time. Civilian employees came over from a nearby unit to collect vehicles from the motor pool and each one was supposed to report in before taking a vehicle. I had a full list and as each vehicle was collected it was signed for and removed from the list. The duty corporal had to check round the vehicles every two hours and on one such round, I discovered that I had lost a tank.

How long I would have had to stay in the army before that was paid off became an unnecessary question when it was found that the man who had collected it had not reported in. He had just driven it away! You might well wonder how it was that a huge vehicle like a tank could have been driven away without my noticing. If it had really been stolen, I would have had great difficulty explaining this to the court martial.

By the time the camp ended, I had spent fourteen weeks in a bell tent, and was not quite as smart in appearance as I had been at the start. Returning to the main barracks to continue working as a drill and weapon training instructor was quite a challenge compared with the rather more relaxed life under canvas, but at least by that time I felt more confident in my role. Very little praise was ever given for just carrying on with the job, but one small incident pleased me greatly. I was working under Sergeant Nicholls who was usually very military and seldom complimented anyone about anything. The platoon concerned was rather smaller than usual, and so only two NCOs were allocated – Sergeant Nichols and me. One morning he was off duty and I had the whole platoon in the barrack room giving a session of weapon training involving the Bren gun.

I was aware that Sergeant Nicholls had entered and had gone into the side room leaving the door open, and I continued with the session which ended about fifteen minutes later. The squad went off for lunch and I joined Sergeant Nicholls in the side room. Normally the platoon would have been divided into two groups for sessions of weapon training – each of us taking one group – so it must have been the first time he had heard me in action. To my amazement, his only remark as he went off was, "You do very well for yourself." Those six words, said with such obvious sincerity, served to increase my confidence immensely, largely because it was so unexpected! Before that, all he had done was criticise me.

The Daily Orders were posted on the board every day at five o'clock. On one occasion three NCOs were directed to join a detachment on the ranges for the following morning. Mine was one of the three names. The men were on the ranges for three days after which they would be transferred to a war zone abroad, and for a while I imagined I would be going with them. As it turned out, the three of us were needed for extra supervision, after which we returned to training. The odd thing was that the men involved were some of the best from their outfit, yet rounds were being let off on wrong targets and mostly wide of the mark, so the general result of the shoot was rather dismal. I couldn't help thinking that many of the men were not too happy about their posting.

On one occasion, when we were on the point of leaving the ranges, the sergeant in charge used up about fifty spare rounds of ammunition to fire, at speed, into the base of a tree. The trunk was about fifteen centimetres in diameter. He succeeded in felling the tree and was very lucky that the officer in charge had left the area.

A few weeks later all basic training was moved from Strensall. Six different regiments had been merged for the first six weeks' basic training and in future all this training would be conducted at the regimental depots. I was in the East Yorkshire Regiment and therefore I was moved to Beverley with about ten other NCOs. This was very good for me, as I was only about eight miles from home. We still had an intake of recruits every six weeks, but only had two platoons – about sixty men – at any one time. The barrack blocks were centrally heated and the food was rather better, since the maximum number using the dining hall was never more than about a hundred.

I considered that I had been very lucky having a fairly local posting, as many of my contemporaries had been sent abroad and saw very much more of the world than I did. Sadly, some of them were drafted to war zones, where some were killed or injured. I was the only national service drill and weapon training instructor at the depot, all the others being regulars, but by this time, I was more confident and felt much more accepted. I enjoyed a good relationship with the other instructors – Johnny Walker, Ken Johannson and Derek Dransfield –

although one day that friendship was severely strained. I had intended to go home on my motorcycle immediately after parade, and when I looked for my shoes, I found that they had been securely nailed to the barrack room floor just under my bed. None of the recruits in the platoon would have dared to do such a thing, and so it had to be one of my fellow instructors – my 'friends'.

On one occasion, I felt really frustrated, and let out a stream of expletives to express my feelings. One of the recruits looked at me with disbelief and said, "That's the first time we've ever heard you swear, Corp!" This really made me think. It's very easy to fall into the way of being rather free with language. However, if something really dreadful happens, it is totally inadequate to say, "O dear me", and the F-word is used to express total frustration. Unfortunately, a good number of the army personnel used it more as a punctuation mark, in every sentence uttered.

Long after I left the army, I dropped the end of a heavy barrow hard on my foot. I emitted the loud expletive within the hearing of James, the vicar's elder son, who was helping me. Going round the corner, I discovered him helpless with laughter. I apologised profusely and explained that when I took off my wellington, I was convinced it would be full of blood. I felt sure he had heard the word before, but not from my lips, and it took some time for him to control himself!

I was at Beverley Barracks when King George VI died. The entire staff and recruits at the depot were paraded at eleven o'clock, and the commanding officer read out the news in what must have been a standard script. It ended with the words, "The King is dead. Long live the Queen!" He then walked off without another word. I thought that it would have been nice if he had said a few words of his own to add some humanity to his statement, but he didn't.

It soon emerged that a detachment of eighteen NCOs and men were to be included in the King's funeral parade, and the list included me. We had a full week excused of normal duties, were issued with new uniforms and were drilled every day by the Regimental Sergeant Major, particularly in practising the 'slow march', which was not included in the basic drill. We all spent much time getting our new uniforms into shape and I thought that we would have looked far smarter wearing our number one uniforms, since they were much better ironed than the new ones issued. Really sharp creases cannot be achieved in such a short time.

We travelled by train to London and duly arrived at Woolwich Barracks where I discovered that the mattress on my bed was really damp. I have no doubt that things were much worse in the trenches, but I chose to sleep that night on the springs of the bed. We were awakened early enough to be on the parade route by 4am and we spent much time moving backwards and forwards, so that the whole parade was correctly spaced out. Ken Johannson and I were side by side in the ranks. As we waited, he kept passing me the small bottle of whisky he had brought. A friend indeed!

We moved off at about 9am, and the actual parade began shortly after. I felt that it was a great honour to be included, but the only time we had a glimpse of the gun carriage carrying the King's coffin, was briefly as we marched past the railway station. The King was being taken by train to his final resting place. That evening, I was spotted 'on the telly' in the newsreel, along with the rest of the detachment from Beverley.

The most unusual incident I experienced occurred about a month after the move to Beverley. We had been on the range for the day and, before returning to barracks, it was the job of the duty officer to check that no man was in possession of any bullets (rounds). The platoon was paraded, and as the officer walked along the line, each man had to state, "No live rounds or empty cases, Sir." I had just returned to the barrack room after the evening meal, when a single shot rang out. One of the recruits was sitting on his bed with his rifle across his knees, shaking like a leaf. It turned out that on returning to his bed space after his meal, he had found his rifle cocked (ready to fire). He had pointed his rifle to the floor and pulled the trigger in all innocence, since when cleaning a rifle and replacing the bolt, this was standard procedure. He had to be put under arrest and marched to the guard room!

The man involved was decidedly quiet and inoffensive. On being questioned, it was obvious that he knew nothing of a round being in his rifle ready for firing. The conclusion drawn was that someone else had discovered a round in his possession, after all the others had gone to lunch, panicked, put it into the nearest rifle he happened to see and closed the bolt. The barrack room was an upstairs one, and after the bullet had passed through the floor, it had ricocheted around the room below. It was really lucky that this particular barrack room was unoccupied at the time! Someone could easily been killed. During the enquiry which followed, it emerged that before leaving the ranges, a few of the men had been missed making their statement to the officer about not having any live rounds, and nothing else was heard about the matter.

After about four months at Beverley, I was awarded a second stripe, thus becoming a full corporal. The only downside to this was that I was then involved with guard duty overnight, every ten days.

The reputation of newly-appointed commissioned officers holding the rank of second lieutenant, varied markedly. Some of them were first class, but others were as useless as I had been when first appointed a lance corporal. The regular NCOs referred to them as 'educated idiots'. This was not to their face, of course. One such officer was involved on a barrack room inspection, with one or two other officers with me bringing up the rear. The young officer came over to me, and said in rather a high pitched voice, "Corporal, look at that man's top kit. It's all higgle-de-piggledy!"

How I managed to stop myself from laughing was a miracle of self-control. I could imagine his nanny, years before, saying to him, "Quentin! Look how you've cleared your toys – they're all higgle-de-piggledy." But I had never heard the expression used between adults.

In August 1962, I was due to be discharged in time to begin my college course in September. Before that, I was interviewed by the commanding officer who actually tried to persuade me to sign on as a regular soldier. This pleased me greatly – much better than being given the idea that they were glad to be rid of me – but my future had been decided. Like all conscripts, I had to continue in the Territorial Army for a while longer. Straight away, I had to attend the fortnight's TA Camp, which that year was to be in the North Yorkshire Moors at Fylingdales, and I was given permission to travel to camp on my motorbike. The fortnightly camps were graded, and this one involved duties in the morning with most afternoons and evenings free. I made a short holiday of it, and was able to be in Scarborough by one o'clock on ten days out of the fortnight.

I was sharing a tent during my fortnight at Fylingdales with five private soldiers. As I was making up my bed for the first night, I suddenly became aware that all five of them were watching me. It transpired that none of them had ever been camping before. The basic rule when sleeping on the ground is to arrange that there are as many blankets under you as there are on top. When the blankets are folded in the form of a sleeping bag, the warmth from your own body is retained above, below AND at the sides. It would never have occurred to me to even mention it, but I'm sure they all slept more soundly as a result of my impromptu tutorial.

On a subsequent fortnight when I was sent on a signals course in Kent, I ran into Ken Johansson. He was at the same camp for just two weeks on another course, so on most evenings we were able to get together and catch up with each other's news. We had been good friends at Beverley Barracks and he was in the regular army. Over the years, we kept in touch and he achieved the rank of Warrant Officer before he ended his service. At one stage, he was awarded the Queen's Medal for Gallantry. When he told me the story, he was suitably modest, and made the incident seem to be 'all in a day's work'. However, the truth was that he had acted very bravely when faced by an excitable man with a loaded gun, and had disarmed him without anyone being hurt.

On my third fortnight in the TA, we were transported down south and part of the training there was spending four days 'digging in' on Salisbury Plain. We were part of a larger operation, and our main activity was to dig several trenches, which were partly covered over and supposed to shield us from an atomic attack. As with all such exercises of this kind in which I was involved, we were never given the 'big picture', which would have made it more interesting. However, in all the activities in the TA, I have to admit that the food was very good, following the saying that, 'an army marches on its stomach'.

On the whole, however, I was disappointed with the apathy exhibited by those involved with the TA at that time. The one incident which completely destroyed my own enthusiasm was a lecture about mines. The general aim at that time was to have not bigger mines but smaller ones. The thinking behind this was as follows: If troops were advancing, and one man stood on a large mine, there would be a huge explosion; he would be blown to bits, followed by silence. If, on the other hand, he stood on a small mine, it would merely blow his foot off, and the sound of his screams of agony would have a much more demoralising effect on his comrades than a mere explosion. I could not imagine the mind-set of an individual who worked that one out. War is never a relaxing exercise, but I regarded this thinking as being totally abhorrent.

It was very shortly after this particular weekend that cuts were made in the manpower level of the TA and I had the opportunity to end my link with the army. I would not have missed the experience for anything, but in many ways I had 'moved on' and did not have the same interest any more. My particular 'move on' was starting teacher training college, which was to be a totally different experience.

Tailpiece: In general, I am a fairly peaceable character – a live-and-let-live personality. The only animals I have ever wanted to kill were ones who greatly offend my lifestyle, such as slugs, snails, rats, mosquitos, and any creature which, given the chance, would tear me to pieces. On the battlefield, the main aim is to kill or be killed and none of us knows how we would react to that situation. Even though I worked very hard in the army, and enjoyed it all, I felt that being a soldier was not really in my nature.

CHAPTER 4
Teacher Training College

When I applied for entry as a student at Borough Road College, Isleworth, in Middlesex, there were two reasons for my choice. Firstly, it was an old-established college with an excellent reputation, but also I wanted to be well away from Hull so that I would not be tempted to go back home too much at weekends. Since the college was about twelve miles west of London, I would be well away from home and, apart from the distance involved, I would not be able to afford to return all that often. I started at Borough Road College in September 1952, along with just over a hundred or so other students. It seemed to me that we were a very mixed bunch, but the college authorities must have seen some spark in each of us, because I believe only one of every three applicants secured a place there.

The lecturers, too, were quite a varied body of men, each specialising in one or two of a variety of subjects. My specialist subject was physics, and there I had really struck gold, because the physics lecturer, Mr Hanson, was a real professional. He was not so much a lecturer as a teacher and he had the skill to really inspire his students. He was also very human and approachable, and was a role model of what I would like to be in the future, not at a college, but in a school. His lectures were backed up by excellent blackboard work so that when we were taking notes, we knew very well that if he left a space on the board, it would be filled, so that the lecture was totally complemented by his layout. One of his lectures was particularly well illustrated, and at the end, he stood back saying, "And that, gentlemen, apart from the physics, is an excellent example of blackboard work!" He was not bragging – he was merely stating a fact – and we gave him a suitably respectful and totally sincere round of applause. Good blackboard work is part of the effectiveness of a good teacher, and over the years I have seen plenty of examples of both good and bad.

Mr Hanson always wore a bow tie, and we each acquired one, which we all wore one particular morning. He walked into the room, paused briefly while looking at us, and proceeded to the podium. His only comment was, "Well, gentlemen, at least mine is not a clip-on."

Years later, I discovered he was living in Wimbledon, and so I phoned him. When I visited him he was ninety-seven years old, but he still had the same engaging personality and I really enjoyed talking with him again. I felt pleased that not only did he have children of his own, but grandchildren and great-grandchildren. Their photographs adorned his walls, and I felt that he would be much loved by them all. His wife had died two years previously, and it was obvious that he missed her very much, but he took great pride in telling me about his family. We exchanged Christmas cards for the following four years, and then his daughter wrote to tell me of his death. I wrote back to tell her how much he had influenced me and how much we had all respected him.

Each of the lecturers had a totally individual manner and ability. The most 'off beat' of them all was Mr Perry whose specialism was art. I saw some of his work and it seemed to me that it was of a very high standard indeed. However, each year he submitted a piece of his work for the summer exhibition at the Royal Academy and each year it was rejected. He took pride in this, until one year an entry of his was accepted. In order not to spoil his record, he withdrew it immediately! His clothing was informal in cut, but highly individual in colouring, and he always wore a black beret with a silver star at the front. The mid-day meal in college was formal, starting with a Latin grace and the lecturers sitting at 'high table'. Mr Perry always finished his meal in good time, and then stood until the principal nodded to him, at which point, he would bow and retire to the pub over the road.

Another very individual lecturer was also rather eccentric in appearance. One of the students had to submit an essay to him in connection with the Divinity course. He copied out the complete diocesan letter of a Bishop, where the topic exactly corresponded with the subject in hand. It was returned to him with the assessment of C-minus and the comment, "Very woolly thinking!" In one of his lectures, he stressed the need for the teacher to get the complete attention of the class. When asked how he would achieve this, he said that perhaps he would ride into the classroom on a bicycle and pretend to fall off. I feel he would have been completely useless as a teacher, and really wondered how he had achieved his job in the first place.

However, we were shown several examples of lecturers actually teaching a class, and one which stands out in my mind was by Mr Kemp. It was a poetry lesson and the poem he used was *The Highwayman* by Alfred Noyes. The class was held spellbound, as were we who watched the lesson; it could have been made into a short training film! Another excellent lecturer was Dr Smith who sadly died about a year after we left the college. In one of his lectures he impressed on us how important it was that all information given to the children was totally accurate. He had a young family and apparently one of his youngsters had gone home with some fact she had been told at her primary school. Dad knew that what she had been told was completely wrong. He was faced by the information that Miss Somebody had told her this, and that nothing he could say had any effect on the truth of what the teacher had told her. In the end, and in desperation, he said, "Look dear – Daddy TEACHES the teachers!" Even this did not impress her, but the story certainly supported the idea that young children believe every word that the teacher says!

One day, in the depths of winter, a sort of challenge went round the college for anyone prepared to stand up to his neck in the Thames, wearing just swimming trunks. It is difficult to understand how this sort of stupid challenge ever reached the light of day, but three students volunteered. The whole student body put up a small sum of money each and the student who stayed in the water longest would win the lot. The total inadvisability of this was that one of the volunteers had asthma, and we had all quite recently returned to college after the Christmas break.

On the appointed day we all marched down to the Thames, which was about a mile from the college, and as we passed a school, some of us appreciated for the first time that teachers can have a sense of humour. When we passed one of the classrooms, all the children crowded to the window laughing and pointing, and the class teacher was in the middle of them also much amused. As we all gathered along the bank, it seemed that at least one of the national newspapers had been informed of the folly of the whole idea, and a reporter was there taking notes.

The college authorities had also known about it and Dr Page, the deputy principal, arrived and informed the three volunteers that any of them who put even his big toe in the water would be sent down (thrown out of the college). As the whole project broke up, it was discovered that one of the competitor's clothes had been smuggled away, but luckily he was offered a lift in a car, to be reunited with his clothing on returning to college. The prize money was divided between each of the three students since all three were prepared to suffer and had given us a very entertaining afternoon!

This activity could be arranged for an afternoon because the principal considered that each student should work in the morning and evening and that each afternoon should be regarded as free time. Apparently, in the afternoon, our concentration is at its lowest.

During each of the summer terms, we had a 'Rag Week' and apart from this causing much amusement to all concerned, we managed to raise a very large sum of money for charity. The week ended with the Rag Parade, and more fun was had by all. I cannot remember how much money was raised, but I was involved in counting it. Much of it, of course, was in small change and we checked it into a large trunk. When the job was finished, it took four of us to lift it!

Not all the college lecturers were conscientious. One in particular seemed to put up a notice fairly regularly to indicate that he would not be present for his lectures on the following day. On one of these days, three of the students went to the Ideal Homes Exhibition and saw him there with his wife and two young children, one of whom was certainly of school age. However, the majority of the lecturers were effective. Mr Hosker, for example, teaching craft, was a model of inventiveness and had it not been for my interest in science, I would have loved to have taken his course. The music lecturer was also charismatic and many of his 'lectures' were centred round the grand piano in the hall. On several occasions the number of his students increased, such was the interest which he generated.

Brentford was only two miles away from the college, and for several years the first Brentford Scout Group had been kept running by different students from the college. There was a shortage of voluntary leaders, even in those days. I became roped in to this job and enjoyed the experience, even though another reason for me choosing a college so far from home was to get away from my involvement with scouting for a while. However, I did enjoy it, and my main aim in that first year was trying to recruit a parent as a leader. In this I succeeded, and my hope was that as a result, the future of the troop there would become more secure. Once a month, I was involved with the Sunday morning church parade with the Brentford Scouts, which made me late for the mid-day meal. I always received a good-natured round of applause when I entered in my scout uniform!

One of my good friends at college, Mike, ran a scout troop in Woodford, and as he owned a car, he invited me to his home on several weekends. His parents were very welcoming indeed, and the visits were a good break from college life. This fostered another life-long friendship, so that when he and Lillian married, I was his best man, and later on, he was mine. When Mike married, it fell on the middle weekend of the Portobello Scout Camp, of twelve days, and this faced me with the question from the scouts, "If you're the best man, why is she marrying Mike?" Well, it WAS funny the first time.

The college had a scout club made up of students who were already involved in scouting, but it was unofficial. We were allowed to have meetings in the college, but it had not been officially accepted by the students' union. In my final year I was able to make the case for it to be accepted, and in spite of some opposition, it acquired official union status. During the vacation between my first and second year, I organised a week's camp for the Brentford scouts and went back to the London area on my motorbike. We used a campsite in Hove and we had about eighteen boys under canvas. The parents we had recruited came along, and one of my older scouts, Charlie Laing, came down on my pillion. The camp was a success, and I seem to remember that we had quite good weather.

Back in college, on one occasion, I was moved to the sick bay for a while when I had flu, and the college nurse could not have been more attentive if I had lost a leg! Some of my friends visited my bedside bringing a lovely daffodil, and it seemed that when Colin went shopping for this, the exchange was as follows:

Colin: "May I have a daffodil please?"

Shopkeeper: "You mean a bunch of daffodils."

Colin: "No, just one!"

Shopkeeper: "But we sell them in bunches of twelve."

Colin: "But they can't GROW in a bunch of twelve. There must be odd ones."

At this point, the lady appeared to appreciate the situation, and with the beginning of a smile she said: "Are you from the college?" He had to admit it and was given the one daffodil.

But he presented it to me in a very nice jam jar.

One teacher I knew described the staff at his school as the most disparate group of people who could possibly work together under the same roof. I feel that could aptly describe the staff at my college. However, the best of them were very good indeed – pleasant and talented.

The main college building was on four floors and the two top floors provided the sleeping accommodation for those of us 'living in'. Each of the bedrooms was sectioned off with the dividing walls being about eight feet high and the fire escape had been dismantled before I started there. This bothered me, so I acquired a long stout rope and kept it on top of my wardrobe. My immediate friends would 'pull my leg' about this but I merely said that if the place did catch fire in the night, they would all be flocking to me! However, the whole idea was based on the assumption that the fire would not start very near to my room.

There is just one more aspect of college life which will seem unbelievable to present-day students; there was no bar in the college. From time to time, dances were held and each time a request went to the principal for us to have a bar. The request was always refused, and this was despite the fact that most of us were two years older than previous intakes of students, since we had completed our two years National Service before we went to college.

I had been at school with the girl who later became, 'The First Lady of Fleet Street', Jean Rook. At the time when I was at Borough Road, she was studying at London University, and I invited her to one of our dances. Academically, she was streets ahead of me, but she was a good sport and we had a pleasant evening along with two of my friends – Eric Wilkinson and Peter Stockdale – who also came from Hull. After the dance, they both came with me to see her off at Isleworth station, and it was quite a while before I lived down the mirth which was caused by the view they had of us going along the platform, with me tailing behind with her case.

During my time at Borough Road, the Queen's coronation took place. There was much activity on the day before the event, and in the afternoon any student who would be spending the night on the parade route could go along to the kitchen and make up his own packed food for the following day. It seemed that most of them would be going to central London to establish a good position along the route and camp there for the night. Even though I am a royalist, I thought they were mad, but when I toured the college at about six o'clock, it appeared that I was the only student still in residence.

I was definitely the odd one out, and so I went to ask matron for a pack up. She was rather irritable and asked why I hadn't presented myself earlier with all the others. She was not the most endearing person at the best of times, but she made a good array of food available for me and when I offered to help clear up, she replied, "Oh, go on with you", in a very friendly manner.

I knew exactly where my friends were positioning themselves and took the last tube from Osterley station to join them just before midnight. Very few of us had much sleep and the atmosphere became more downbeat as the night progressed, but when it was announced over the loudspeaker system that Edmund Hillary and Sherpa Tensing had climbed Everest, the whole crowd erupted, jumping up and down and cheering wildly.

The news had obviously been held back so that it was the first item to be released on the day, but it was certainly very well timed. As the parade passed, Winston Churchill received a good round of applause, but an even louder greeting was given to Queen Saloti of Tonga, a very ample lady with a huge smile. She was waving enthusiastically to right and left and obviously enjoying every minute of it. Despite the fact that by then it was raining, she left her carriage open so that she was getting soaked, and this, too, was appreciated by the crowd.

The ending of college life seemed to be very abrupt, in just the same way as when my spell of National Service had finished. Life seems to fall into 'chapters' and when one ends another starts. There are certain abrupt changes which take place in life, and from then on everything is different. However, I was never in any doubt that I had taken the right course and this is the other characteristic of starting a new chapter: you know when you're doing the right thing.

Tailpiece: When my time at college was drawing to an end, I considered taking an extra year to achieve a further qualification and I approached Mr Hanson to ask his advice. I had achieved quite good results in practical teaching during my school practice and he obviously knew of my fairly average academic ability and his advice was, "You will learn far more about teaching during your first year in a classroom, than you ever would by continuing as a student." How right he was! The other factor was that I was looking forward to having a real salary once a month.

CHAPTER 5
Fountain Road Boys' School

So... childhood, school, army service and college all behind me, I was now embarking on a further chapter of my life – being appointed to my first school as a teacher. At that time, there was no question of applying for a particular school; you were directed by the local authority, and I was allocated to Fountain Road Boys' School. The building had been erected almost a century previously. In some cases the fathers of the pupils, and even the grandfathers, had attended the school. The six main classrooms were positioned alongside the main hall, and there were two outside 'prefab' buildings. One of these provided two classrooms plus cloakroom and toilets, and the other contained the woodwork room and technical drawing room, again with cloakroom and toilets. The age range of the pupils was six to fifteen years and there was no streaming except in the fourth year, when there was the fourth year class plus the 'scholarship' class, about which, more later.

At the time, I was pleased to have been appointed to any school, but the gloss of my enthusiasm was rather tarnished when a friend's mother asked which school I had been allocated. The lady who asked was rather 'upper class' compared with my own very ordinary background and her response of "Oh!" seemed to indicate that she had hoped for something better for me, Marlborough, perhaps! I was delighted to have been appointed anywhere.

On my first visit I climbed the stairs which led to the only upstairs room in the whole place. There I met Mr Rowland, the headmaster, who was sitting in a room, about fourteen feet square, which served as the head's room, the staff room, the secretary's room and the first aid room. He had an authoritarian air about him. Although he smiled, it seemed that his face was not really used to the experience. It was only later that I appreciated how hard he worked and that underneath his stern exterior he could be very human and caring. During my time in the school, I learnt a great deal from him and came to respect him enormously.

But this was to come later and in my fairly unsure state of mind, I needed to be careful regarding what I said. I cannot remember much of what was said, but it was obvious to me that his was a 'safe pair of hands'. The only question which I remember asking him was to enquire if the school had a science lab, since science was my specialism. He replied that there was a science cupboard, and I resisted the urge to ask him how many pupils this would accommodate. It was obvious that humour was not very high on the agenda. I was not given a tour of the school, but was told that I was to be form master of Class 5, with other classes for some science lessons plus nature study and RE, with some of the younger children.

On my first morning there, Mr Rowland took me to meet my class, and indicated to me which pupils I should have as class monitors. "You want Adams and Prescott", he said. There was no question of my having any part in the decision, but, as in many directives, he was right. The main thing I remember from my first year was the constant appearance of Mr Rowland in the classroom and even hovering outside. The complete left-hand side of my classroom was made up of glass panels, with the pupils' work displayed on the lower part. It seemed to me that most times when I looked across in that direction, Mr Rowland's eyes could be seen travelling across from right to left or the reverse. It became obvious that he was keeping an eye on me.

All the exercise books of each subject were withdrawn at intervals not only for the work to be inspected but in order for him to check that the marking was up to date and I particularly remember one batch. Mr Rowland came into my classroom after four o'clock with a set of books and as we both sat down, he placed the pile between us. Indicating the top book by tapping it urgently with the back of one hand, he said to me, "What's this?"

I restrained myself from giving the obvious answer but on looking more closely I could see that the boy concerned had been tracing the outline of a 'pin-up' on top of the book so that the outline was impressed on the book's cover. I glanced sideways at him hoping to detect some hint of a smile but this was not forthcoming, and so I said, rather shakily, "Ah! It seems to be something of a pornographic nature." There was a pause. "It is! It is!" he said very intensely. "What are you going to do about it?" Again, I glanced towards him, hoping to see a smile, and once more, being disappointed. "I don't really know", I said. "Well", he said, "take the book home tonight and if you warm the handle of a spoon and rub it all over the outline, you can remove the impression." I can usually see the funny side of most situations, but sadly, Mr Rowland didn't. The boy was a really pleasant lad and he obviously had good taste.

Under Mr Rowland's influence, I learnt more about being a teacher than I had ever learnt at college. Early in my first year, he said to me, "You like the children too much. You have to learn to hate them before you can like them." I could not understand this at all, but later I felt what he meant was there should be some distance between the children and the teacher. I was not there to be liked, but to stand a little to one side and be their mentor. However, I never fell into the trap of courting mere popularity. I was there to do a job.

I had a fairly ancient BSA motorcycle on which I used to get to and from school and, usually, it was reliable. However, one morning on my way to school, the chain came off, and replacing it took some little time. I was late for school with hands covered in oil and at the morning break I was having my leg pulled by the staff. In my defence, I said that this was the first time that I had ever been late. In the silence which followed, Mr Rowland remarked that this was more times than he had ever been late for school in his entire life. I felt duly chastened!

Each week, the boys were marched to the Beverley Road Baths for swimming and once the boys were changed, they lined up along the side of the pool for foot inspection. None of the homes had a bathroom and it was not unusual for several pupils to be told to shower and wash their feet. Years later when I was thinking about this, I could not imagine making any pupil suffer the indignity of even having his feet inspected, let alone being sent off to wash them. However, by that time the pupils I taught all had homes with bathrooms, and having foot inspection was a thing of the past.

One day, when I was marching my class to the baths, I encountered Mr Rowland walking towards us. To my dismay, he ignored me and turned my class straight round again to return to the school. That day they missed their swimming. I felt that this was a criticism of me not keeping them in order and also that it was rather unprofessional of him. It was the only time I felt belittled in front of the children, but I took good care not to let it ever happen again.

On Friday mornings, Mr Rowland took the whole school in the hall for half an hour, and the staff was allowed a little time off in the staff room. If I had to return to my classroom for any reason, I had a front view of all the pupils through the glass in the hall door. They were sitting cross-legged on the floor, with all eyes riveted on Mr Rowland and, apart from his voice, silence reigned. I used to marvel at this in my first year, and could never imagine that I would ever have the ability to exercise such an influence.

Another incident which illustrated Mr Rowland's control of the pupils happened in my first year. The boys had all filed quietly into the hall for morning assembly. Mr Baker, who played the piano, moved to his chair, and under the gaze of Mr Rowland and the entire school, he sat down. At this point the chair fell apart; I have a picture in my mind of every joint in the wooden chair coming adrift so that Mr Baker was left sitting on a heap of firewood. No one laughed!

Standing alongside my class about half way up the hall, it was all I could do to contain myself. I have always had the ability to see the funny side of almost any situation, and on that occasion I was sorely tried, yet again. Mr Rowland went across to help Mr Baker to his feet, nodded to a boy on the front row to fetch him another chair from the nearest classroom, and the assembly continued as planned. I would have loved the discipline in the school to have been good enough for us all to have a laugh – including Mr Baker who was not hurt in any way – and then for the assembly to continue, but again, humour was not on the agenda.

I taught one class of six-year-olds for a period of nature study and I found this really difficult at first. Although I had learnt the names of pupils in my own class, it was only very gradually that I managed to learn the names of the pupils I taught for only one lesson a week. The problem was brought home to me when one of the boys in a front desk was obviously day dreaming and gazing into the middle distance. I snapped my fingers in front of him and said, "Are you with us?" He came to earth looking quite surprised and (I swear this is true!) answered, "Yes, Sir. Jimmy Withers." I think he was surprised that I appeared to know his name at that early stage and I could think of no reply, but he did pay attention for the rest of the lesson.

The biggest success I had with this class was when I took in four grass snake's eggs, and with the entire class looking on, two of the eggs hatched out almost on cue. For the first two months or so, I had difficulty keeping the attention of these younger ones, and in my mind blamed their class teacher. In fact, I soon discovered that he was excellent and I was the one who sometimes fell short of holding their interest.

I was younger than the other teachers on the staff, but I found that they were all supportive in helping me to integrate into the team. However, anyone looking at the playground duty rota would know that I was a 'rookie'. The card with my name on it was pure white, whereas the remaining cards were various shades of grey depending how long each had been at the school.

One of the staff helped me greatly on my very first day. The toilet seat adjoining the staff room had a half circle of metal fixed at right angles to the underside, and if the seat was left down when the toilet was flushed the result was a minor flood. His special post of responsibility seemed to be to warn newcomers about this. I never found out why the metal had been fixed there in the first place! His other interest appeared to be buying all the Sunday newspapers and filling in the various competitions which they contained. Apparently he had a vast array of items won in this way and was very proud of his achievements. He was quite a small man, and the other thing I remember about him was that, one day, when he was using the guillotine, he inadvertently sliced off most of his tie. It says much for his amicable nature that he laughed along with the rest of us in the staff room.

During my first term, I was visited by one of the local inspectors. He arrived at the end of the school day, and so we were in an empty classroom. The blackboards were freshly cleaned and he started with a stick of chalk at the left, filling the space as he talked, so that by the time he finished, all the boards were filled with his notes. After he had gone, Kenny Gardham returned for something he had forgotten. He studied the blackboards for a short time, and his only comment was, "By 'eck", at which point he smiled at me and walked off.

Kenny was quite a character, and one morning when I ran over the corner of one of the flowerbeds with my motorbike, he saw what I had done, and quick as a flash was on his hands and knees moving the soil about to remove my tyre marks. Turning to me, he remarked, "We mustn't let Mr Rowland see this, Sir!"

On yet another occasion, a boy had wet himself, and Kenny took charge immediately. Fetching a cloth, he said, "I'll mop it up, Sir." He was a very popular boy, smiling and friendly, and I would love to meet him again. He will obviously have changed in appearance, but I'm sure he will not have changed in temperament.

Each day, the pupils and some of the teachers from the girls' school came over to us for lunch and we had the chance to meet them. One of the stories told to us was when the PE inspector came to visit them, and took over the lesson in the hall which served also as their gym. She was what might be described as, 'quite a character', being extremely enthusiastic and demonstrative.

She was rather like a version of Joyce Grenfell (the famous comedienne of the '50s and '60s). Among her instructions was, "Stand up straight girls and show us your buttons!" After she had left the hall, one of the girls said in a very bemused tone, "Isn't she FUNNY, Miss!" At this point the inspector had returned and had obviously heard the comment, so hoping to save the day, the teacher said, "Yes, dear. But she's very nice."

As my first year was drawing to an end, Mr Rowland informed me that the following year, I was to be in charge of the scholarship class. No post of special responsibility (or extra income) was linked with this move but much more work was involved with coaching the brighter boys. However, I was pleased that Mr Rowland considered me fit to do the job, although I felt there would have been no rush if it had been, 'up for grabs'.

Rather fewer than half the boys would actually sit the scholarship examination, and there were papers on maths, English and intelligence. Each year, only a small handful from Fountain Road succeeded in going on to a grammar school, but they were all given the best possible chance. We even coached the boys regarding the questions in the section on intelligence, and I believe that by coaching in this way, the IQ result could be improved by about five or six places. On one occasion, there were letters to the local paper concerning one of the questions, namely, 'In the series, O,T,T,F,F,S,S,–,–,–, what are the next three letters in the series?' It was deemed to be a trick question and was therefore disallowed. (In case you are curious, the next three letters are E.N.T. – it is a number series, not a letter series.)

The boys in this class had been well drilled in their previous year regarding drama lessons. When the time came for this, I stood back amazed while they all moved desks clearing a space for the stage. When the whole operation was completed, two boys remained in the middle standing back to back. When I asked what they were doing, they were rather indignant that I should have to ask. It seemed that they were the curtains and before any action took place, they moved solemnly apart, turning round to face each other indicating the curtains were fully drawn back.

The facilities there were rather basic. However, film strips could be borrowed from the education centre for a week at a time. The snag was that none of the windows had proper blinds, so that if I wanted to use a film strip in the afternoon, I had to get eight old blackout curtains which had to be trapped at either end of two top windows in each bay. Proper blinds may be drawn in seconds, but trapping old blackout curtains in this way and acting quickly to fix each corner before it fell away, could use up half the lunch break! Taking them down was much easier, but then each one had to be properly folded and stored away for next time.

This year, I was in one of the 'prefab', classrooms, and saw rather less of Mr Rowland, which led me to think that perhaps I did not need to be kept under quite so much observation as before. The class consisted of forty boys of varying academic ability, and for some subjects, they were in 'sets' to make allowances for this.

The saddest incident of my time there was when one of the older boys stole a plane from the woodwork room. He was 'found out' almost immediately and, on being questioned, it seemed that he came from a large family and everything in the home was shared. All the clothing was washed and stacked in a heap in the airing cupboard. The toys were all shared in the same way, and all he wanted was to have just something which he could call his own. Needless to say, he was not punished in any way, but I happen to know that he did end up with one or two things which he really could call his very own.

One boy in my class had poor backing from home and I discovered his mother had died some years previously. In the summer of my last year at Fountain Road, he joined the scout group to which I was connected. He attended the summer camp, and at the end I ran him home to discover that his father was in gaol, and the outcome was that he would be taken into care. I talked to the local authority official who was handling the matter and asked if the boy could come to live with me until his father was released. I feel sure that a request like this would not be allowed today in such an off-the-cuff manner, but the official readily agreed and I took care of him for three weeks. After he had gone to bed, on his first evening, I washed the blankets he had taken to camp, to discover that after three washes, they were not really grey at all, but much lighter and with a pattern!

Another story which originated from about the same time was that one of the boys went to the local shop to buy a toilet roll. The following Monday, he returned with the toilet roll saying, "The company didn't come after all, so can my mother exchange this for a jar of jam?" The shopkeeper obliged.

Towards the end of my third year at the school, I was contacted by Mr Harrison, who was the Chief Inspector and I was asked to go and see him at the

Guildhall. To my amazement, I was offered the choice of five different schools, one of which I could move to in the following September to teach science. I was completely taken aback. I felt that Mr Rowland must have given me an absolutely glowing recommendation, or that there must have been some mistake!

I asked for twenty-four hours to think it over, which was granted and that same evening I visited a neighbour of ours, Mr Foyston, who was a well-respected headmaster in the same authority. He had known my parents from well before the war and so, of course, he knew me. I told him of my interview and he asked to see the list of schools on offer, four of which were housed in old buildings similar to my present one, and the other that had opened for the first time earlier that same year. He pointed to this one, and with the air that head teachers either have or acquire said, "Tell him you want that one and you're not interested in the others!"

"I can't say that to the Chief Inspector", I said, sounding suitably horrified.

"Of course you can", he said. "He's given you the choice."

He then invited me to jump in his car and he would show me the school. He drove to the Longhill Estate, and we parked in front of East Mount County High School. The place was deserted but I could see spread in front of me a three-storey building with workshops to the left, the splendid entrance to the right and a lawn with rose trees along the front. Pointing along the ground floor of the classroom block, he indicated that the two laboratories occupied most of that floor, with a preparation room between them. However, it was only later on that I was given a complete tour of the school, to find that beyond the entrance hall, there was the staff room, main hall, dining room and kitchens, gymnasium and showers and a sports field to the rear.

"That's the school you want", he said, "so tell him!"

The following day, I mentioned the situation to Mr Rowland, although I thought that he obviously knew about it, and that afternoon, I again visited Mr Harrison to tell him of my decision. Given the choice, I feel sure that he must have known which I would choose, but he merely made a note, and wished me well for the future. I was to find that most of the inspectors were pleasant people.

Tailpiece: And so, my time at Fountain Road came to an end and I left with very mixed feelings. I was looking forward to teaching mainly science in a proper laboratory but I would miss the friendships which had been formed with the staff there. I would also miss the children and the challenge of working in less than ideal surroundings. I had learnt a great deal about class control, and with Mr Rowland as my mentor, I had learnt a great deal about working with a team. This was the end of another chapter, but very obviously, the start of a new one.

CHAPTER 6
East Mount County High School

Compared with my previous school, East Mount County High School was from another planet. It had been open for only two terms and when I started there were eight staff. However, several classes from the junior school nearby were being housed in the same building, as their own had yet to be finished. My initial visit to meet the headmaster was scheduled for 7pm, and the entire school appeared to be deserted. I started walking round the outside and ended up looking through the window of the headmaster's room where Mr Hankinson was sitting at his desk. It must have been something of a shock for him when he looked up to see this dark figure in motorcycling gear, complete with helmet, peering in at him. However, he quickly recovered and with a circular movement of one finger, he indicated for me to go round to the main door. I felt that it had not been a good start.

However, he was very pleasant, and my time at East Mount was to be much longer than I had spent at Fountain Road. As we walked round the school, we chatted generally and I felt much more relaxed than I had been during the first meeting with my previous headmaster. The facilities were an absolute revelation to me and I felt that I had really 'landed on my feet'. I visited the school several times during the summer holiday familiarising myself with the laboratory and the layout of the school and later at the first staff meeting, I was again made to feel very welcome. At some time during my first year, the staff and pupils of the junior school left us when their building became ready for occupation. Relationships between us and the junior school were quite cordial, except that one of their teachers seemed to spend a great deal of time reclining in the staff room and it was rumoured that one of the pupils marked his maths books for him. I feel that this was not necessarily true but such was his reputation.

The classes were streamed, A, B, C and so on, and a few years later when we were in full swing, we had five streams in each year. Form 2A was given the one laboratory then in operation as their form room and so I was their form teacher. I felt quite pleased to be assigned the A stream until I discovered that they were deemed to be the most trustworthy pupils to be based in the laboratory. Streaming related to academic ability and this did lead to a 'them and us' situation among the pupils. It was some time before I appreciated the fact that pupils did mind being in a lower stream. On one occasion, a class was lined up outside the laboratory and, as I walked up, I said, "Let's see now, this is Three A isn't it?" The muted reply came from several pupils, "No, Sir. We're Three E." It was a genuine mistake on my part and I tried to pass it off by saying, "Oh well, you wouldn't be any happier." Again, there were several soft but really sincere voices saying, "Oh yes we would, Sir." I never made that mistake again, but it really made me think.

Even though the number of staff was so limited in the first year, the deputy head, Cliff Jones, and the senior mistress, had been appointed. Although the deputy had quite a sense of humour in the staff room, he seldom let it show in front of the pupils and he was regarded as being strict on discipline. I always thought the title 'senior mistress' was unfortunate, but she too was very keen on discipline. I once witnessed her caning one of the girls and it even frightened me. I never sent a girl to her for punishment, ever again. The senior mistress was also involved with cookery and needlework. On the top floor there was a room laid out like a proper flat with cookery area, bathroom and bedroom and all the furnishings. A few years later, two boys broke into the school one Friday evening and actually lived in the flat for the entire weekend. They had kept it really tidy, as well.

On another occasion, the deputy head was invigilating a written examination based in the flat. The room had been rather cold earlier and he appeared to have forgotten that some of the gas rings had been deliberately left on. Unfortunately, he was leaning back against one of them. The urgent cries of one pupil, "Sir, Sir", were at first ignored, until he realised what was happening, by which time, the back of his jacket was well alight. Amazingly, he managed to slip out of it without harm, flicked the offending garment into the nearby sink and turned on the tap.

He subsequently applied to the local authority for a new jacket and managed to get a complete suit with two pairs of trousers, despite the fact that his trousers had not been damaged in any way.

All teachers have a pastoral role to play, and the balance has to be kept between being regarded as a 'pushover' and at the other extreme being too remote or strict. On one occasion, for the first period of the day, a second-year class filed in and I was involved with a demonstration lesson. By the time they settled to notebook work, I had noticed that one of the boys, who was usually very cheerful, looked rather dejected. As I walked round looking at their work, I bent over him and said softly, "You don't look very happy this morning." To my utter amazement he burst into tears. I led him to the door, turned to the class and said, "You can see Robert's a bit upset today. Just get on while I see what we can do." Youngsters can be really nice at times; he was a typical lad and very popular and they could see that he was really miserable about something. They carried on with their work while I was just outside the door.

It seemed that he had a younger sister who was handicapped and that morning his mother had been so preoccupied looking after her that he had been completely ignored. He had made his own breakfast, got himself ready and left for school, without a word being spoken to him. I talked to him since I had some experience of how much time could be spent looking after a handicapped person. I took him to the head's room and Mr Hankinson rang his mother to tell her what had happened. She came in to the school to see him, and I told the pupils that there had been a little problem at home. When he returned to the class, he was much happier.

Quite early on during my time at East Mount, the school was getting more and more pupils, and the time came that posts of special responsibility were being increased. Mr Hankinson saw me and explained that he was very happy with my work and that there would be a post available, but I was rather young and so he would wait a while before I would be considered. Having thought about this, I went to see him during the lunch break and choosing my words carefully said that if I was giving satisfaction in the job and I was carrying the responsibility, surely I should be considered. I was awarded a post, and eventually made a head of department. I didn't feel clever about this, but it came home to me that I was working under a very reasonable head.

I used to spend quite a lot of time in the woodwork room during lunch breaks and boys would often be given permission to finish off some work there, provided a teacher was present. On this particular day, the chimes of the 'daisy bread van' could be heard as it passed by. One of the boys remarked, "There goes the daisy bread van", and I looked up at the boy who was watching me working and said quietly, "Daisy bread van. Which class is she in?"

Unfortunately, he was not the sharpest knife in the box and his reply in quite a slow and solemn voice was, "I don't know, sir." I looked at him and there was not a trace of a smile so I let it pass and continued with my work. A full minute later he added, "She's not in our class, sir."

I said no more, resigned to the thought, "You can't win 'em all!"

The range of ability in any year group can vary from borderline brilliant to really remedial, and this boy would have been classed by some as being 'thick'. It is completely wrong to cause amusement by making fun of such a pupil, and I never did. Luckily none of the others had heard the exchange, but my attempt at humour had failed on this occasion.

Towards the end of the summer term we always had a full week when the timetable was set aside and an examination timetable operated. This was good training for any of the pupils who were likely to take outside examinations at some time in the future. No lessons were actually taught and whereas my own timetable was normally taken up with science lessons, during that week I might be involved with invigilating any class with any subject. For one session I was invigilating class Four E who were supposed to be writing an English essay.

At the end of the session, I collected all the papers and when the class had filed out I glanced through them. I was dismayed to discover that one boy, who was of very limited ability, had written, 'yonkity yonkity yonkity yonkity', again and again, and had filled half an A4 sheet of lined paper. Not for the first time, I reflected on the limitations of secondary modern education. Clearly the boy needed more individual attention than we were able to give. I can imagine that ten minutes into the exam, most of the class would be writing and he would feel that he had to write something, but he would feel lost.

We had a Polish lady appointed to the staff who sadly had no great control over her classes. On one occasion, I had to go round the school with a message and as I opened the door at the back of her classroom, she was shouting at them above the din, "Za trouble vis you lot, you don't understend plain inglish!" The last two words were shouted at double volume.

Neither she nor any of the pupils had noticed that I had opened the door and so I retreated into the corridor until I could control myself. (It has been mentioned before that I am easily amused.) When I re-entered at the back, the noise gradually subsided and all eyes were on me. I asked permission to speak, swept one of my 'looks' across the entire class, gave out the message, and treated them to a further meaningful 'look' before I left. I felt sure that minutes later the noise level would have returned, but I had to get round all the other classes.

It was a great step forward for me when I discovered that I could control a class, not by shouting, but by giving them a 'look'. Perhaps with my normal expression, I had a head start anyway.

I knew of one teacher who had the reputation that he had once killed a child. He never had any problem with class control but he never made any attempt to dispel the rumour either.

Another teacher had difficulties with class control at first. I was in the entrance hall talking to a colleague when she first walked into the building. We both knew she was starting that day, and she really looked like a lady who would have no trouble with discipline. I made a remark quietly to that effect, and he agreed, but we couldn't have been more wrong. She was middle aged and had done most of her teaching in private schools in India. She had difficulty handling our type of youngsters; on one occasion in the staff room, she said, "When I was teaching in Poona..." However, she was such a lovely person that the pupils warmed to her and although she was never strong on discipline, at least the pupils liked her, and worked reasonably hard in her lessons.

When the senior mistress left to become an inspector in the Lake District, Mrs Booth was appointed in her place. She appeared to be stern and unbending, but she was well-liked both by pupils and staff and below the surface was very kind and caring. As I was writing this chapter, an old pupil, now sixty-nine came to see me and admitted quite openly that he had loved her!

When I thought about head teachers generally I was always sure that I would not like to work in a school with a lady head, which rather marks me out as a male chauvinist something-or-other, but I would have been happy in a school with her at the helm.

Either Mrs Booth or the deputy head would stand at the front of the stage as the pupils entered for morning assembly and one morning she was too close to the edge and fell off. The stage was about four feet high so that she could have been really hurt, but she recovered herself, smoothed her dress, walked to the side steps and across to her original position centre stage. The attitude of the pupils was entirely one of concern. No one laughed. Some at the back craned forward a little, but the impression was that they were all anxious for her and relieved when it was obvious that she was unhurt.

On another occasion, she marched into the staff room, banged her case on the table, and announced to those already present, "This school gets dafter! A pair of shoes has just dropped past my window from an upstairs classroom." In the silence which followed this pronouncement, I remarked, "We ought to feel really thankful no one was wearing them." If looks could have killed, I would have been stretched out on the floor breathing my last, but it was a measure of her humanity that she was later able to laugh about it with all of us.

This incident happened at about the time when I was trying to stop smoking. She would really enjoy her after dinner cigarette, and I would see her open her bag, take out the box, open it, and so on until finally her cigarette was lit, and she would sit back with obvious pleasure. It was agony for me, so I still cannot understand why I stayed in the room at all. My stopping smoking had become rather a joke in the staff room because I had tried repeatedly to give up without success.

One New Year, we all returned to school and I announced in the staff room that once again, I had stopped smoking. It was Jim Griffiths who helped me greatly by betting me ten shillings (fifty pence) that I couldn't keep it up for six months. I was quite determined to get the money from him so I did something to make me even more determined. After three months of not smoking, I bought myself a second-hand duplicator on the strength of what I had saved in the first three months and what I was going to save in the second period. This was over forty years ago and I have never smoked in all that time. But I don't think I ever got my ten bob from Jim.

Around that time in early December, I won fifty pounds on one of my premium bonds. I was stupid enough to make this known in the staff room and someone remarked that I would be able to buy the wine for the Christmas drink on the last day of term. It became a sort of tradition that I would provide the wine for this event and, before I had moved on, I must have spent all the fifty pounds, and more.

In the first few years, the school was taking in more and more pupils as the Longhill Estate increased in size and more youngsters came into our catchment area. The staff numbers also increased, so that eventually there were twenty-seven of us. Miss Walker (Val) and Miss Brown (Ann) formed a firm friendship and, sadly, the object of their activities seemed to centre on me. One lunch time, they took my white laboratory coat and sewed polo mints all around the hem, pockets, collar and cuffs, and simply put it back where I had hung it. I was not going to let it be thought that I couldn't take a joke and so I wore it like that for several days. It caused some amusement to staff and pupils alike, but quite quickly the joke wore thin so I removed them all. (At home, of course!)

One lunch time, four boys arrived late at school, and their story was that they had seen a flying saucer. This was relayed to the staff who were split about 30%/70%. Some believed the story and some were of the opinion that they had made it all up – the majority! Years later, one of the boys concerned came to our house. He was then working for a carpet firm and had arrived to dry clean one of our carpets. I was really pleased to see him, and after a long conversation, I mentioned the story about the flying saucer and asked if it was true. He looked at me in an amused way and said, "Of course it wasn't. We made it all up!"

I had a white van, and one Friday I had it loaded up so that I could have a good start to get away to London for the weekend. Halfway through the afternoon, Val Walker came to me to ask if she could borrow a spanner. This was duly returned to me a little later and when I tried to jump into the front seat of the van, I found it was missing (the seat, not the van!) I stormed back into the school and later I was rather pleased to learn that they had hidden from me in one of the caretaker's broom cupboards. I found the seat behind the gym, so I was only delayed for about half an hour.

Much later, after I had been happily married to Brenda for several years, they told me that the headmaster had sent for them both and said, "Look here, this joking has got to stop or else one of you will have to marry him!" Happily, I managed to make my own arrangements with that!

One Friday afternoon, two ex-pupils, who were clearly drunk, visited the school and they were met by the deputy head who took them into the head's room to humour them. He was having some success and at least keeping them out of sight of pupils who might be changing lessons, when Mr Hankinson walked into his room. Incensed with the relaxed atmosphere which prevailed, in HIS room, and seeing that they were clearly drunk, he made quite an incident of it all, and threw them out. The head and his deputy usually got on quite well with each other!

It would be wrong to give the impression that all was sweetness and light between members of staff, or between pupils and staff. On one occasion, the woodwork teacher was accused by one of the boys of deliberately cutting him with a chisel. After a good deal of questioning, it emerged that the boy had deliberately cut himself and made up the story to get back at the teacher over some punishment which had been meted out to him.

I think many teachers have problems with some pupils regarding relationships, and even now, after I have been retired for nearly thirty years, I always cheerfully admit that I'm still waiting for some ex-pupil to come and punch me on the nose!

An unfortunate incident occurred one Friday evening when I remembered that I had left my own 16mm projector at school, and I needed it for the following evening at home. I parked my car outside the school and, having no key for the main gate, I climbed over. Reaching the main door, I used my own key to get in, recovered the projector, and came out locking the door as I left. I climbed over the main gate straight in front of a policeman!

I explained that I actually worked at the school, I had the key for the building but not for the outer gate and the projector was my personal property which I had left at school by mistake. Amazingly, I was believed, but I suspect that since the school was part of his 'patch', he may have recognised me.

I have attended several reunions of old pupils, and found them all friendly and appreciative of their schooldays. At one such gathering, when I always try to have a word with each individual, I sat next to this particular man who was well turned fifty. After preliminary introductions he said to me, "My word, there was one time when you gave me a right rousting!" I pretended to edge away from him and said, "Would it help if I said I'm sorry?" With great forcefulness, he said, "No! I deserved it!"

On meeting old pupils I have found that almost invariably they had enjoyed their time at school and were not resentful regarding any punishment they had been given. Perhaps I have just been lucky. On the other hand, the ones who had hated school would not be among those who attended a school reunion.

I remember one boy who could be a real pain, but although he was a nuisance, he was very likeable. On one occasion, when I was talking with his mother, she told me of an incident when she had 'grounded' him in his bedroom.

Later on, she had gone back into the room, and he was sitting on the upstairs window ledge with one leg outside and one inside. "I'm going to jump!" he shouted and his mother was so fed up, she shouted, "Get on with it then!" Of course, he didn't.

On his last day at school, he came to me and said, "When I'm twenty-one, I'm going to come to your house and take you out for a drink." I never got the drink, but he did come and see me, and he had not changed at all. Regretfully there are some pupils, both boys and girls, who are totally unlikeable. I would try harder with such pupils, but often it was a lost cause. I used to think sometimes that their parents were perhaps disappointed with them. A good teacher will try to treat all pupils equally, but it must be admitted that, as with adults, some are just more likeable and pleasant than others.

When an evening event was held at the school, the caretaker would patrol round the outside of the building at regular intervals. On one occasion he walked down the side of the gym and, at the corner, a boy was looking across the field. He was so engrossed that the caretaker was able to walk right up behind him and was able to see what activity the boy was finding so interesting. Another boy and a girl were engaged together on the ground with the girl's clothing in great disarray. When the boy realised that the caretaker, too, was watching the proceedings, he said reassuringly, "It's OK, Sir. It's me brother!" The caretaker was having none of it, and sent them all packing!

Teachers come in all shapes and sizes and with a range of abilities. One teacher I knew had the philosophy that, as teachers, we're all just child minders. He would develop this premise whenever he could muster an audience. We all recognised him as a very good teacher indeed and knew he didn't really think that at all. However, he had one talent which I think is so essential for a good teacher: he had a great sense of humour.

In my last few years at East Mount, a fifth form was created of pupils who were above average academic ability, but who had nevertheless failed the scholarship examination. Many of them benefitted from this extra chance. After two or three years, one successful pupil returned to see us, and was actually handing round cigars to male members in the staff room.

I had a small group who were taking physics with chemistry, and each week I had them for a full afternoon. The first hour was devoted to 'chalk and talk', and the second was for practical work. During one particular day I had a dental appointment over the lunch break. I had decided that as one of my front teeth had been broken and capped when I was much younger, I would have both front teeth removed and have a plate made for just the two front central teeth. The plate was already made so that when the front two top teeth were extracted it could be put in place immediately. Now a plate takes a little time to become used to and, as I went back to school, I was aware that my speech was not quite normal. The science group were also aware of my problem and were exchanging amused looks with each other.

After a few minutes, I decided to come clean and tell them how I had spent my lunch break. I answered the inevitable questions, and then carried on with the lesson without further amusement on their part. I doubt if I would have got away with it with younger pupils, but the science group were all staying on at school and they all wanted to learn. I even think some of them may have thought that I was quite brave!

The music teacher at East Mount was Mrs Ivy Campbell. Not only was she a good teacher, but it seemed that every weekend she made herself a new dress. Two of the male staff kept a tally of her record and noted that on thirty consecutive school days, she had worn a different dress every day!

She was also responsible for producing the annual drama evening, which was always a musical. Ivy demanded a very high standard, and on one occasion a friend of mine visited the school after four o'clock and looked in on one of the rehearsals. He was very impressed, although at one point one of the girls had to stand near a stage tree. Ivy shouted to her several times to stand nearer to the tree, and he remarked to me afterwards that if she had been any nearer the tree, she would have been up it!

Most of the staff helped with the productions in various ways, and my own contribution was to act as stage manager. It was quite a wide stage, but we were able to paint one scene on the back wall and then I arranged for two separate backcloths to be lowered in front so that three different scenes could be used for each production. More than half the ladies on the staff were involved in making costumes, those with skill in painting dealt with the backcloths and each production ran for three nights with a full house each evening. I remember that they were of a very high standard indeed.

Eventually, when I had been teaching at East Mount for more than ten years, I had almost become part of the furniture. Several of the teachers in other schools who had been in the same class with me when we were pupils, had become deputy heads and two had even become head teachers. Although I was happy at East Mount, I had allowed myself to get into rather a rut, so I began to apply for promotion. I was successful at my third interview and I could not have been more pleased, but at that point, I began to think how different life would be for me.

As a deputy head, I would not have a full teaching timetable, but would be involved with administration and seeing parents much more on a regular basis. The schools in Hull were on the point of being reorganised, and 'middle schools' were being introduced. However, this would have overtaken me anyway, because my present school was to become East Mount Junior High School the following year with an age range from 9 to 13 years.

My departure from East Mount was rather low key because the headmaster was retiring at the same time. I was presented with a framed picture which I had been able to choose. However, after the last assembly, I was sorting out one or two last minute items in my room and was intending to say goodbye to Mr Hankinson, when, through the window, I could see him leaving to go to his car. I had to run after him to wish him well, and he had obviously not been intending to have a last word with me.

By that time, I was one of the longest serving teachers in the school and I can remember being disappointed in him. And he had only been at the school a mere two terms longer than me! After he retired, Mr Hankinson taught part time as a class teacher in another school, and one day when he was on playground duty he came across a group of boys smoking 'behind the bike sheds'. When he caught them at it, one of the boys said to him, "Why don't you just push off and leave us alone like the other teachers do?" I wish I had been there!

Tailpiece: At East Mount, I progressed from being the youngest member of staff to being one of the longest serving teachers. In any situation where several people work closely together, there are disputes from time to time and this school was no different. I have found that when up to half a dozen adults work together, relationships are usually excellent, but as staff numbers increase, it becomes more and more likely that 'factions' emerge. In general, it was a happy staff at East Mount and the degree of co-operation between most staff members was very high indeed. However, even teachers have a personal life, so at this stage, I feel something should be written about that.

CHAPTER 7
Family Matters – It Certainly Does!

For years I went through life never imagining anyone of the female persuasion would fancy me. Much later, when I had time to give the matter some thought, I imagined that being unattached for so long, I was too selfish and settled in my ways to be a good husband. In the event, once I had taken the plunge, it didn't seem such a bad idea, and in fact I have been brilliant! But to be serious, Brenda and I first met when she had been asked to help with serving the lunch to a group of scout leaders who were on an adult leader training course. We were both leader trainers in the county, but up to that point we had never actually met. Each of us knew everyone else involved, but she was concerned with training Cub Scout leaders and I was involved with Scout leaders.

Brenda and me on our wedding day.

She said, "You must be Phil Brock", and I said, "And you must be Brenda Hebblethwaite." It was all very romantic. At that time, shorts were the order of the day for boys and male leaders, and Brenda always said that she had fallen in love with my knees. How salacious does it get?

When I was younger, my self-assessment was very low. Link that with the fact that I was heavily involved as a leader in a large scout group, and it would have to be admitted that I would be a very poor catch for any lady. With this in mind, I hesitated for quite some time, but when we finally decided on getting married, we soon became engaged and the wedding followed only four months later.

Just before this, Mike Speed, a good friend of mine, was staying with us for a long weekend and I had seen an attractive house for sale in Bilton Village. On Monday morning, when Brenda had gone to work and Mike was intending to return home, he asked to see the place and we drove over there. We parked in the road immediately outside the house and, as we were looking, the lady of the house opened the front window and beckoned us in. She showed us all round the house and we were halfway round the garden when she turned to me and said, "You ARE the man from Scotland, aren't you?"

When I admitted that I was not the man from Scotland, whoever he was, she was filled with embarrassment, but I assured her that Brenda and I were looking for a house and we thought she had been very kind. As we walked away, Mike turned to me and said, "For goodness sake tell her you want it."

As the asking price was about 50% more than I would ever have imagined we could afford, I had to talk to Brenda first. The following evening, Brenda and I both visited the house. It was a cold September evening and they had a log fire burning in the lounge. It was really snug and cosy and Brenda liked it at once. Mr and Mrs Borthwick were emigrating to Canada and were anxious to be off. They were both really pleasant and the following Saturday afternoon they showed us round the half acre garden, which also had a piggery building with facilities for eight breeding sows. Mr Borthwick took me to one side and told me that his wife had 'taken a shine' to us and she really wanted us to have it. This could have been salesmanship, but I felt it was genuine.

The entire garden was under cultivation with lawns front and back. There was no boundary fence between our house and next door and the lawns extended across both the properties. Before we left, we indicated that we would like to have it and arrangements were put in place straight away. The house was ours before Christmas.

Brenda and me early in our marriage – looking older already!

For some time, Brenda and I had been seeing each other regularly, but there was no possibility of our moving in together. It would have been regarded as 'living in sin' (this was over forty years ago) and our mothers would not have been able to face the neighbours. I was living on my own in 'our' house, but I was not really concerned about this. I had lived with my family for more years than most offspring, but earlier, I had bought a houseboat and had great fun and a fair amount of help in renovating it. I lived in it on my own for about six months, after which time, the novelty had worn off and I went back home again.

However, even though I still had reservations about being a half decent husband, we decided to get married. We had a meal together with both pairs of parents, and were amazed how the conversation flowed. They had known each other, or known of each other for years, and the links which emerged were amazing. At one point, Brenda and I went into the kitchen to fix the next course, and both of us felt that we could just clear off and leave them to it!

Brenda's younger sister also attended, and although she had been in a wheelchair for most of her life, she could certainly hold her own in the conversation. I was then living in 'our' house and Brenda visited very regularly, but as we look back on the situation it seems totally ridiculous. We never spent a night together until the day we were married. When you think about it, it's not sleeping together which causes problems, it's staying awake together!

By the time we got married, we were both well-turned thirty, and it caused much hilarity among our friends when they learnt that the reception was to be held in the Darby and Joan Club in Cottingham. On the Saturday before the wedding, all our friends at the Portobello (Methodist) Scout Group gave a party for us involving over a hundred people, and we really appreciated that. We were married at Willerby Methodist Church, which was Brenda's Church, and her 'Uncle Bill' – Rev. Arnold Jones – conducted the service. His son (Brenda's cousin) played the organ and composed some music especially for the occasion, all of which was also really appreciated. And so we embarked on married life. We wanted to have a family and there was just one time when we thought we'd made it, but it was not to be. We had been involved with youngsters for most of our lives, but we were never very upset about not having our own. We just got on with life.

We had a fancy dress party on New Year's Eve for about 8 years running. I am in the centre with Brenda on my left.

At about this time, the television series *The Good Life* was running, and one of Brenda's friends remarked that Brenda had always reminded her of Margot, played by Penelope Keith, but since our marriage, she had become more like Barbara, played by Felicity Kendal.

Brenda and I both worked in the garden and we kept chickens and later, turkeys. I had always wanted to keep pigs, but we decided that we had quite enough on our hands without something extra to be looked after. We grew a whole variety of vegetables and fruit bushes, and planted several hundred small Christmas trees for growing on. We had a greenhouse and later we built another one, so we were able to grow about a hundred tomato plants.

At that point, both of us were still working, so we would leave several bags of tomatoes and an honesty box in the outer veranda when we went off to work. Only once was the cash short which rather disappointed us, but the following Saturday, a lady came along with the money. It seemed that on the Wednesday she didn't have any change, but she really needed the tomatoes. We also grew several different varieties of flowers and Brenda would call in with them to Humber Street on her way to the bank where she worked.

One Friday, I had a phone call from my mother. She and my father had moved to live in Scarborough when he retired at sixty-two and they'd had five happy years there. Mother always used to say that every day was like a holiday. Unfortunately on this particular day, she was there on the line to tell me that my father had gone into hospital following a heart attack that morning. I had known of many people who had recovered from this and were still living full and active lives, so I tried to reassure her and said that I would come over the following morning.

I knew he had been trying to break up an area of concrete which had been the base of an old shed in the garden, so the following morning I drove over, armed with a fourteen pound hammer and other gear. It was my aim to have the concrete completely broken up in the morning so that we would be able to report this when we visited him in the afternoon. At about midday when Mother and I were having lunch, the telephone rang. Sadly, it was the hospital to say that my Father had suffered another more serious stroke and they had been unable to save him.

Mother had always impressed me with the way she dealt with emergencies. She insisted that we visit the hospital to collect his belongings, and made other arrangements before she left Scarborough to come back with me to Bilton. In my father's little workshop, a piece of wood had been left in the vice and he had obviously started a job which he would have hoped to finish. He never did. Things could have been so different between us, but it was too late. Life can be very cruel.

Brenda was away playing badminton somewhere in the West Riding, so she knew nothing about all this. She returned home on the Saturday evening to hear the sad news, by which time, Mother was asleep. She wanted to move from Scarborough immediately, but I persuaded her to stay on for a while. I imagined that if she moved back to Hull, she would regret leaving Scarborough. However, she was determined to return to be nearer to Hull, and Brenda was instrumental in finding her a bungalow just round the corner from us. As soon as she saw it, she liked it, and Brenda helped her to buy carpets and curtains and so on.

Mother had a good friend, Sadie, who had lived next door to them before they moved to Scarborough, and she proved to be a tower of strength. Before Mother moved back to be near us, Sadie went over and stayed with her for several days at a time; later they visited each other very regularly and Sadie even came on holiday with us.

A few years later, when Mrs England next door sadly died, her house came up for sale and we were able to buy just over an acre of the field adjoining her land. We wanted to build a bungalow on it, but there were several snags to be overcome and not least of these was the fact that the parish council was greatly opposed to the idea. By this time we were selling plants and shrubs, and they imagined that we might be trying to start a sort of garden supermarket on the land. In fact, we were hoping to have a nursery, but it was never our idea to make it a huge project. However, we eventually obtained planning permission for the bungalow and were able to go ahead.

The area was a much neglected field with a bomb crater near the far end which had degenerated into a very dirty pond. In 1941, an enemy bomber was being chased off and the remaining four bombs were dropped so that the plane could get away more quickly. There were four ponds which mark the direction in which the plane was travelling and ours was the last one. These lie in a line roughly north-east of our pond and, sadly, the first bomb to be dropped killed several people in an air-raid shelter immediately in the path of the plane.

Planning for the bungalow had been carried out over about five years, mainly when we were on holiday and we had a great deal of fun altering the design. When we were ready to apply for planning permission, we asked an architect friend of ours for advice. Over a period of two hours, he dismantled our plans during the first hour and then put them all back together in such a way that it was still exactly what we wanted. However, it would then stand a much better chance of being accepted. We actually ended up with one upstairs bedroom and the main hall extending to the roof, with a balustrade and walkway on three sides.

We had designed the bungalow so that, if the need arose, my mother would be able to have the small downstairs room as a bed-sit. In the event, she was very independent and active, and after my father died, she had fourteen more years, as she met up with old friends and she still played the piano regularly. She always said that life was never the same, but she certainly made the best of it.

Brenda's sister, Betty, was really bright, with a ready wit, wrote splendid letters and did excellent needlework. However, she had been handicapped from birth, due to her having cerebral palsy. Her parents had devoted their lives to looking after her and so we both appreciated that, eventually, her care would rest with us, and more particularly, with Brenda. Eventually, her mother and Betty both moved into our downstairs bedroom.

When we finally obtained planning permission, Brenda had retired from the bank, so it was she who acted as 'clerk of works' for the building. We sold our house around Christmas time, before the bungalow was finished and we were pleased that our good friends, Jean and John, were able to help us. Jean's mum had just moved into care, and we were able to live in her flat until our bungalow was finished. Much of our gear had been moved into the old piggery building (now updated), and the family who bought our house let us use one room temporarily to store our main items of furniture. When we moved in, our belongings didn't have to be moved very far, and some of our friends helped with the job, so this was completed in well under half a day. We then sent out for fish and chips for us all.

On the same day as we moved into our bungalow, which we called 'Evergreens', the death of a friend was reported in the paper. He and I had been scouts together as boys and he was only fifty-one. We had always intended to have a small in-ground swimming pool, but we decided that it would have to wait two or three years until we had recovered a little from all the expense of building the bungalow, but following this sad news we had a digger in the following Saturday!

I had not yet retired, so work on the pool could only be done on evenings and weekends. When we concreted the base of the pool, there were eight of us, two on each of the three concrete mixers and two spreading the concrete over the metal rods which formed a honeycomb over the base. The work took a whole day with Brenda supplying food and drinks, and each helper received a certificate entitling them to life membership of the 'Brenda and Phil Brock Leisure Complex'. One of the helpers was Mike Pittaway, who was an ex-pupil from Neasden JHS, and I'm sorry to have lost touch with him. Whenever old pupils come to see us, they are invariably friendly. Mike and two or three of his friends came to the pool the following year, and we had several visits to the beach.

View of the gardens from our bedroom window.
Everything in place for an Open Afternoon.

The pool was finished and ready for use in the first week of the school summer holidays. Brenda and Chris were the first to actually swim in it since, when it was ready, I was at Pocklington with the school camp.

Once the bungalow had been built, and the pool put in, we were able to go ahead with developing the land, and although a good deal of work still remained to be done with the bungalow, making the surrounding land reasonably presentable took far and away longer. Many people imagine that we had an overall plan right from the start, but the truth is that it all happened in a very haphazard way. We sorted out a bit here and a little more there, so the reason that it hangs together so well is more by good luck than good management. We developed a little at a time, but the first job was turning the bomb hole into an ornamental pond, and with this we had much help from Chris and Dave. There is a full account of this in another chapter.

The 'bomb hole' pond near the end of our gardens,
It now has a fence around it – Health and Safety!

Of course, we made some mistakes. Some trees were planted far too close to each other, many of which still remain, but we are proud of the fact that we planted every single tree on the site. Now, after over twenty years, the garden alone covers about half an acre and we are trying to make it a 'fun' area, with features to make people smile. We are also trying to make it child friendly and youngsters certainly enjoy the play area which was developed about three years ago.

When two or three children arrive with their parents and run to the bottom of the garden, they are usually heading for the tower. This was built in the very early days, with much help from Chris and Rob, and Rob's brother, Geoff, who built the first arch. Even today we are still making alterations and improvements, some of which are linked with trying to make the garden more manageable.

However, back then, no matter how much we worked on the garden and in the house, we were always mindful of the fact that our main responsibilities lay with our families, and Brenda had more responsibilities in that direction than I did.

Sadly, Brenda's father had developed cancer, and eventually he went into the Nuffield Hospital in Hull. The care he got there was second to none and when we visited the nurses were really kind. After he died, Brenda spent at least one night a week supporting her mum and Betty and this soon became two nights and, eventually, she had to spend more time with them than with me.

Mention must be made here of Nick Matson and Richard Hare. These two became weekend boys in the garden centre and, at the time when Brenda was away looking after Betty and her mum, they proved to be good friends as well. They stayed at Evergreens for many weekends and Nick even came to France with me twice. We always went on holiday with friends and, at the time, we used to join Jean and John, with their teenagers, Lynn and Steve, on a campsite at Le Gurp. Later, when Nick was about eighteen, he went to the College of Art in Hull for a year, and as his family lived out of town, he stayed at Evergreens from Monday to Friday every week during term time.

However, eventually, Betty and her mum moved in with us and sold their house in Willerby. As planned, they used the downstairs bedroom, which also had en-suite facilities and they settled in really well. Betty had no great sense of pitch, but she would often be singing in the bathroom early in the morning, "Oh what a beautiful morning, Oh what a beautiful day, I've got a beautiful feeling, everything's going my way!" It made me feel ashamed at some of the trivial things which I allowed to 'get to me'. About this time, we brought a *caravette* which had been specially adapted with a wide door at the side. A hoist had been fitted and Betty could be raised to the floor level inside while she was still sitting in her wheelchair. The chair could then be wheeled in, and secured in place, so that she could have a splendid view through the large windscreen and the windows at either side.

We have two other good friends, Debbie and Terry, and Terry agreed to deal with fitting out the interior so that Brenda and I could use it for holidays. Terry was great for two reasons – he was a skilled joiner and also his work at the time involved fitting out static caravans. My function was definitely as his assistant and with his advice I was able to do quite a bit of the work in the evenings and during the week.

For several years, in the summer, we rented a cottage near Bridlington for a fortnight and our mothers, Betty, Brenda and I would have a holiday together. Each day, we would go to some place of interest in the *caravette*, and we all really enjoyed this break. Later on, we had to have carers to help with things and these ladies soon became personal friends. This allowed Brenda and me to spend some time going out, just the two of us, and even have a holiday on our own. On one occasion, when they were still living in Willerby, Chris's mum moved in with them for a fortnight so that Brenda and I could go off somewhere on our own. She even took them out in her car and the whole arrangement was *really* kind of her.

We had a great deal of extra help at the time when Betty and her mother were with us, but about a year ago, we decided that we needed some help ourselves. That was the time when Coral entered our lives and she came strongly recommended by one of our previous carers. Coral comes for four two-hour visits each week. Earlier in the year, when Brenda had been in hospital, her help was invaluable and the time rapidly came when we didn't want to do without her! We look forward to her visits, and when Brenda decided that she really didn't want to drive anymore, it was Coral who volunteered to drive her to Hornsea each Saturday in her own car. Brenda has a number of friends who meet at the sea front cafe and now Coral has made friends with them all. Hornsea is a special place for Brenda, since her family spent some time there during the war, to escape from the bombing in Hull.

After Mother returned to Hull, she lived over fifteen more years, and met up with her old friends (the girls, even when they were turned eighty). However, one day when she was nearly eighty-four, she rang us to say she felt unwell. We shot round there in the car and collected her and she spent the day with us. After tea, she perked up a bit, but it was decided that I would stay overnight with her. Brenda came across with me and helped her into bed, then went home, and I did one or two little jobs in the kitchen. No more than five minutes had elapsed before I looked in on her again, and she had died!

This was a huge shock for us, because up to that time, she had shown no signs of slowing up at all. However, when things had settled down, we both thought this was exactly the way we would want to die rather than being on a bed of sickness for weeks, or worse still being in pain. This thought sustained us, but didn't erase the sadness.

In time, Brenda's mum became too ill for us to look after her, and she had to go into care, where we visited her regularly. Sadly, her condition deteriorated and eventually, she also, died. This was very sad for us, but much worse for Betty, because they had been together from Betty being born. But the plain fact was that she was not enjoying life by then and in the end, it was a release. We still had to have carers for Betty, and many of her friends came to visit her. She always loved company. Brenda and I were not getting any younger and it took both of us to lift her in and out of the bath, mainly because she thoroughly enjoyed her meals and was quite a weight to handle.

Finally, it was decided that Betty would go to live at Saltshouse Haven, about a mile away from us. We suffered agonies thinking that she might feel rejected but, on Brenda's first visit, Betty's immediate reaction was, "I love it here!" She just enjoyed being with people, and had settled, even at that early stage.

It was a great place, and the attitude of the matron was, "These people have chosen this to be their home, and we must make it so." Her room was the first one on the right of the entrance so that everyone visiting went past her door and gave her a greeting. She had eight very happy years there; Brenda visited her every day and took her out in the *caravette* two or three times a week. There was just one day when she was 'off colour' and she died that same day at about teatime.

She was over fifty years old, and the fact that, as a person with cerebral palsy, she lived so long was largely due to the care which she had had from her parents and from Brenda. It was also because she made friends very easily, she was a fighter and she was invariably cheerful, in spite of her handicap.

All the staff were crying and very much upset by her death, and Brenda immediately started to make arrangements for her funeral. Although Brenda was so upset, the arrangements were started the same evening. The first question was who would lead the funeral service, and the obvious choice was Brenda's cousin

Colin and his wife, Jill. When they were young, Brenda, Colin and his sister Hilary, and Betty had spent much time together on many occasions, not least when their parents lived in Whitby where their father was a Methodist minister. Colin knew Betty really well, and his wife was a local preacher. They were pleased to conduct the service together, and it was all very personal as a result.

Our good friend Margaret Gibson, who had been a tower of strength as one of Betty's carers, came with us in the funeral car, as did Vicky and Rob. Two ladies from Saltshouse Haven came along to the service to represent the ones who had been close to Betty there and, although it was all sad, it was good to know she had touched the lives of so many people.

Brenda and I were now on our own, and we had achieved many of the things we had wanted to do. Over the years, we had had some really good holidays, including visits to New York, Florida, Canada, China, Brazil, The Netherlands, The Canary Islands and, of course, France and Spain. We had also visited Australia and New Zealand to see my cousin John and his wife, and Talia's wonderful family on the farm in Te Puke near Auckland. We've been very lucky!

Although this is supposed to be my life story, Brenda has played a great part in it. We met as a result of our involvement with the Scout movement. She ran a cub pack in the Willerby Carr Lane Group and later became the Assistant District Commissioner for Cub Scouts in the Haltemprice District. She worked for the National Westminster Bank and, as a result of her being an Associate of the Institute of Bankers, she became the Branch Accountant in the office. This was the first time that a lady had held this position in the North of England. Brenda subsequently became a Magistrate on the Hull Bench, and later became the Chairman of the Family Court Panel.

Tailpiece: As I write this, I have now reached the age of eighty-one although Brenda is considerably younger (only eighty!). Most of our life is now behind us and we are unable to do some of the things we did when we were younger. However, we are well aware that life does not go on forever and we are not worried about dying, BUT there are still many things that we would like to do in the future. We have always had many good friends, which is surely one of life's greatest blessings.

So, now on to the next stage of my career...

CHAPTER 8
Dulverton Junior High School

My new school was Dulverton Junior School, the first school to be built on the Bransholme Estate. The reorganisation in the Hull Authority was to take effect from September of the following year so our age range at that time was seven to eleven years. When the estate was completed there were to be six junior high schools or middle schools.

We opened with the head (Basil Dale), the deputy (me), and just three staff members, so that for the first year, I was a class teacher taking all subjects. After having a full timetable taking science for over ten years, this was a real challenge. We started the year with 140 pupils and since the houses were all still being built, a day seldom passed without a new pupil being admitted, and often there were two or three. New members of staff were being appointed periodically as the pupil numbers increased and this also made life more difficult.

I had met Mr Dale at my interview, of course, and even at that early stage, he indicated that I should call him 'Bas' – in private, of course! Within a few years, a degree of informality of this kind was not uncommon, but I found it quite unusual at first. However, I discovered that he was keen on camping and had been running a school camp in the summer holiday for several years, so immediately we had one interest in common.

Although the school actually opened as a junior school, within twelve months, it was to become Dulverton Junior High School or Middle School, with the age range 9 to 13. Most of the heads and deputies in the junior schools had to re-apply for their jobs, and many of the older ones decided to accept early retirement, but in view of the fact that Mr Dale and I had been appointed so recently, we were excused having to re-apply. During the summer holiday, I spent quite some time familiarising myself with the layout of the building which was unique in our local authority, and receiving much of the equipment and books that would be needed on the very first day of the term. Another building was being erected, which happened in all the smaller junior schools that were to become junior high schools and it was known as a conversion unit.

This was a very basic structure which provided a woodwork/metalwork room, a science laboratory, an art/pottery room and a facility for domestic science. The last two areas were in one large room, and later we put in a partition wall to create two separate teaching areas. This was done on a DIY basis, and when the Chief Education Officer came to the school for a meeting, I pointed it out to her. I was disappointed that she seemed barely interested. I consider that it should be one of our aims to get parents interested in the school. After a year or two, the term conversion unit lost its significance and we then referred to it as the practical block.

The number of pupils in the school increased steadily, and when we reached the stage where we ran out of spare classrooms, a temporary classroom was installed at the side of the main building. Before eight years had elapsed, we had four temporary classrooms dotted about. Towards the end of my time at Dulverton, plans for a proper addition to the facilities were in place, but this was not implemented until I had moved on.

Quite the most stupid occurrence during my eight years there was when the secretary received a phone call, which went like this:

Caller: "I've just rung to let you know there is a bomb in your boiler house."

Secretary: (Who had been busy with some administrative jobs.) "Good! Thank you very much."

It was only after she put down the phone that the content of the message really registered, and she came dashing to the head's room, where Mr Dale and I happened to be having a deep discussion about some aspect of school life (drinking tea). Looking back, I can hardly believe what happened next. What would two responsible adults do? Would they (a) clear the school; or (b) ring the police?

We both went straight to the boiler house to investigate!

Now in our defence I must claim, (a) It would seem very unlikely that some maniac would ring and give warning of such an event; and (b) the boiler house was well away from the classrooms, being separated by the kitchens, the dining room and the main hall, all of which were empty. Luckily, it turned out that the phone call was a hoax. However, if the warning had been genuine, the local authority might well have had to advertise, 'Replacements are required for the Headmaster and the Deputy Head of Dulverton Junior High School, due to unforeseen circumstances'.

The general atmosphere in the school was splendid. When we started, there were just two year groups. When we were in full swing, there would be four year groups, but we opened with only the first and second years. After a year, we had a new first year intake and the two existing year groups moved up. This happened the following year as well, so that the original second year were the 'top' year group for three years.

Rumour had it that the first few hundred families to be moved into the new estate were all selected as having 'good' backgrounds – free of crime, no previous history of rent arrears, and a good record of taking care of their children and their houses. We certainly believed this to be true, since all the early pupils admitted seemed to be pleasant and well cared for.

Although Mr Dale was really excellent at dealing with most situations he would have been the first to admit that he hated giving first aid in the event of an accident. On one occasion when we were in camp, two boys were digging a hole and one of the boys put his hand in the hole just as the other boy was bringing down the spade. The unfortunate boy had a finger chopped so that it was literally hanging off, and Mr Dale immediately passed the boy over to me. I took him to the clinic in Pocklington from which point he was transferred to Hull Royal Infirmary and the finger was successfully stitched back. However, he must have been in some considerable pain and he took it very bravely.

On another occasion, Bas and I were talking to each other in his room when a boy came to his door quite agitated. "Sir! Sir!" he said sounding really desperate. "Now that's very rude", said Bas, "Mr Brock and I are talking." The boy had the attention of both of us and he then removed his hands which had been both placed together in front of his trousers. At this point, he revealed the fact that he had caught his manhood in the zip of his flies.

Now it was Mr Dale's turn to sound desperate. "Oh, Mr Brock, will you deal with this, please?" he said. I took the boy next door to my room, and found that the zip was only slightly caught, so that no blood was actually flowing. When he was released, he had no pain and I was able to reassure him that no real damage had been done.

* * * * * * * * * * * * * * * * * *

On the day when decimalisation was introduced, we had been issued with a full batch of thirty centimetre rulers and our instructions were that the new rulers had to be issued immediately and all the old twelve-inch rulers had to be sent to the boiler house to be burnt. This was duly carried out.

That same day, I asked two of the boys to help me move a cupboard during the lunch break. It only needed edging along for a very short distance. Looking underneath, I said to them, "That's nearly right – just another inch." One of the boys glanced at me with a mischievous look on his face, and said, "What's an inch, Sir?" The twelve-inch rulers had only been withdrawn that very morning!

One problem which arose was really trivial in a way, but I felt that I had to get to the bottom of it. Each day, two of the girls were detailed to sort out the washing up from the staff mid-day drink. One of the ladies reported that 50p had disappeared from the pocket of her outer coat and since the staff room was at the end of a long corridor, they were sadly the chief suspects. (You may well wonder why a teacher would need to carry 50p in the pocket of her outer coat.)

I sent for the girls, put the situation to them and invited them to explain. I tried reasoning; I tried being Mr Nice Guy and finally came on to them quite heavily. At this stage, one of the girls said quite loudly and with injured tones, "You've no right to talk to us like this, Sir!" I stood behind my chair looking at the floor, and in all honesty wondering what to do next. In the silence which followed one of them said, "You won't tell me Mum, will you, Sir?" I could have hugged her!

The 50p was returned and I immediately became Mr Nice Guy again. If I had told their parents, it would have blown the situation into a much bigger drama and their parents would have been disappointed with them. As it was, the lesson had been learnt and it was never mentioned again. But I should have told their parents.

Every classroom had a huge built-in cupboard with loads of storage space. There were two main compartments, the lower one being about six-feet high and the upper one about two and a half-feet high, and the total length of the cupboards was about ten feet. The upper cupboards were fronted by two heavy sliding doors, each with a solid wooden frame. The weight of each of these doors would be about the same as the standard front door of a house. On going back to my classroom one lunch break, I discovered that one of the top doors had parted from its groves and was lying flat on the floor. If it had fallen on to a pupil, the child would most certainly have been killed. Needless to say, all the high cupboards in the school were then checked over to ensure that such a thing could never happen again.

Mr Dale was a master at story telling. Every year, in the run-up to Christmas, he read *A Christmas Carol* to the pupils and he had them hanging on his every word. He spread the story over several morning assemblies and he was brilliant. We used to have a Friday afternoon assembly and again he always had some sort of story. One week, we were expecting the only black boy we had ever had in the school on the following Monday. He spent some time talking about this, and asking them to make him feel welcome. He asked them to imagine how they would feel if any one of them was going to a school where all the other pupils were black.

Unfortunately, one of the boys had been absent on the Friday afternoon, so he missed that assembly. At break time on the Monday, this boy greeted the new lad by saying, "Now then, chocolate face." I feel sure he intended it to be in fun, but the new boy was crying and upset. Needless to say, Mr Dale was almost as upset about it as the new boy himself, but he dealt with the situation so that afterwards they were both friends.

On one occasion, we acquired about half a dozen large pumpkins, and the cookery teacher arranged for groups to make pumpkin pies, and make enough for every pupil in the school to have a piece so that each of them could find out whether or not they liked it.

We bought an incubator for chicken eggs, which had a transparent top and held about twenty-four eggs. Mr Dale lived outside the city boundary and he was able to contact a local farmer who supplied him with fertile eggs suitable for hatching. Each one had to be turned every day so a cross was marked on each egg, and the pupils arranged that on one day, the cross would be on top and the next day is was on the underside, and so on. This is done to prevent the yoke from sticking to the inside of the shell which would cause the developing chick to get stuck. When a chicken sits on a group of eggs to hatch them, she will carry out this move herself.

On day twenty-one, as the eggs started to hatch, every pupil was able to watch for a short time to see an egg being pecked from the inside and the chick eventually emerging, damp and tired. They were then able to see that within a very short time when they dried off and the feathers fluffed up, they were able to scramble about and peck. Since the eggs all started to hatch at different times of the day, these stages were seen by every youngster. We took the pupils half a class at a time, which caused some disruption to the timetable, but we felt it was well worth it.

Several pupils had mentioned that they would like to attempt the Lyke Wake Walk. This activity involved walking more or less west to east from Osmotherley to Ravenscar, covering forty-two miles over rough moorland. This route is where the monks used to walk and has its own history, but the hike was very popular as a challenge in the 1950s and 1960s. After a while, with such a track being made that the moorland was being eroded, organised groups were banned.

When the idea was mooted, there were about twenty of our fourth year – both boys and girls – who wanted to have a shot at it. Now this is not the sort of activity to be entered into lightly, and a great deal of planning was needed, plus adult help as backup. The normal plan was to start at about 9pm on the Friday evening, so that when dawn breaks, the rest of the walk can be covered in daylight, and then completed within twenty-four hours. Since this involved walking at night, it was usual to choose a time when the moon was full.

The pupils were well prepared and at the final meeting on the Friday, before we set off, we stressed again how important it was to have adequate and suitable clothing. When it came to question time, one pupil asked how many of them did I think would complete the entire walk. I hesitated in giving an answer, but when pressed, I said that I really didn't think any of them would complete the full walk, but it would be very good experience for them. On previous occasions with parties of adults and older scouts, I had seen any number of strong and healthy older boys drop out around the halfway spot – Ralph White Cross – looking absolutely shattered. I felt that I had to be honest so that none of them would be too disappointed if it happened to them. But it also occurred to me that perhaps some of them thought, "We'll show him!"

I could fill several pages with more details, but briefly summing up I was really impressed by their spirit and determination particularly as they were in the 12 to 13 age range. About six or eight adults, some with cars, formed the support group and check-points were established along the route where food or soup was available so that they could have a rest before they moved on.

EVERY PUPIL COMPLETED THE COURSE, AND ALL OF THEM DID IT IN WELL UNDER 24 HOURS.

I felt really proud of them all.

The following year, some of the new fourth year pupils wanted to have a go at it as well, and the local authority, having had time to consider the possible danger, informed us that they would not sanction it. We were all very disappointed.

In every year group, there are always some pupils who make more of an impact than others. One pupil made a set of chess pieces of the main characters in the government at the time, and the main ones in the opposition, using *papier mache*. He painted them, and the whole idea was really inventive. He was also involved with a short film involving animation. When he went on to the senior school, rumour had it that he was involved in some sort of production entitled *Robin Hood and his Gay Men*, which was immediately banned, and it thoroughly annoyed the headmaster!

By this time, Mr Dale and I had been at the school for nearly eight years; we had experienced more than our fair share of problems and were both ready for a change. Mr Dale was hoping for a bigger school, and I was considering applying for a headship in a comparable school. In the event, we were both successful, he to a bigger school and I was appointed as head in another middle school, both to start in the September of that year. The local authority was able to appoint a head to replace Mr Dale in September, and Mr Horsley who was on the staff at Dulverton was appointed Acting Deputy Head. There are always misgivings about 'moving on,' and although I had really enjoyed being at Dulverton, I was looking forward to the challenge of actually running a school.

We were both given a good send off by the staff and the pupils, and then quite suddenly, rather like this chapter, it was all over!

Tailpiece: As the junior high schools were established, there was an air of anticipation that the age range involved was a great idea, and we were able to introduce pupils to specialist teaching gradually. For the first year, the teaching was mainly class based and specialist teaching increased year by year. Dulverton JHS, in my opinion, now had too many pupils for a middle school and the school where I was going had about half that number.

CHAPTER 9
Neasden Junior High School

The school had been open for nearly ten years before I arrived and the headmaster was Don Shaw, a well-respected and experienced head. We had met several times at various meetings. He seemed pleased that I was the one who had been selected to follow him and he was retiring for a well-earned rest and, hopefully, a happy retirement. He was a local Methodist preacher and was always ready to come back to lead an assembly, which he did on a regular basis. I always made him feel very welcome and so did the pupils. Shortly after he retired, I rang him, only to hear the voice at the other end say, "Hello! Neasden Junior High School here." For a second or two I was lost for words, but then I replied, "I don't think it is, because I'm here." He laughed heartily and remarked how old habits die hard, but I felt that he missed the children, and the school, even though he had been pleased to hand on the responsibility.

I can still remember going back to my room after I had conducted my first assembly, sitting back behind my desk and thinking to myself, "What have I done?" The moment soon passed and from that point I never had any regrets about accepting the challenge. This is not to claim that I never made a mistake. I was far too soft, for example, on any member of staff who was too confrontational with me. I always believed in trying to make allowance to individuals, but after I had retired, I could see that this was interpreted as a weakness on my part.

Very shortly after I had been appointed as head at Neasden, it turned out that one of the fourth-year pupils lived next door to the head of another middle school. We were good friends and he told me, in a mischievous way, that he had asked the boy what he thought of his new headmaster. He might well have been expecting the boy to say, "He's useless!" or some such remark, an assessment which I'm sure would have been passed on to me in fun, but with great gusto. The boy had in fact replied, "He's strict, but fair."

I was surprised by this comment, because I didn't regard myself as being particularly strict. However, after thinking about it I decided that I could live with it. After all, I was not there to be popular, but to do a job. It alerted me though, to the fact that perhaps I was a little, 'on edge' with my position and still feeling my way.

The dividing line between being respected and being feared is a very difficult balancing act. I wanted pupils to know that they could come to me with their problems. I was well aware that some of the head teachers I knew would never be approached in this way. However, I did have a cane and used it when I thought it was necessary, although I must admit that I could not do this to a youngster now. The two offences I was particularly concerned about were a pupil smoking in front of younger pupils or being cheeky to a teacher. I knew of one head who was nicknamed 'Mr Next Time' by staff and pupils alike. When a pupil was sent to him for punishment, he received a telling-off followed by the threat, "Next time it will be the cane!" Discipline in a school is vital but I didn't want pupils to think that the only reason they came to me was for punishment. Looking back on my time as a headmaster, perhaps I did overdo the idea of being too readily accessible to pupils.

An older boy who came to me certainly presented me with a problem. It seemed that he had bought an air pistol but his parents had told him to get rid of it. His question was would I look after it for him until he was sixteen, at which point he would come back to me and reclaim it. Clearly, parents should always know what is happening with their son or daughter, but here was a boy who was putting me in a position of trust. It was not an easy decision, but I decided that I would do it. Had the parents known what I did, they could well have assessed me as being 'out of order', but I agreed to it and took the pistol. And the boy did come back to me when he was sixteen to reclaim it!

A friend of mine, who I will call Mr Walton, was a senior member of staff at a high school where he was faced with an even greater problem. The incident concerned a boy who was in trouble with the police and he had gone 'on the run'. Some of his friends from the same school were still in contact with the boy and he had asked them to find out if he would agree to meet Mr Walton. The rendezvous was to be Mr Walton's car one lunch time so that they could talk.

This was duly arranged, with just the two of them, and Mr Walton talked with him for a while. He strongly advised the boy to give himself up, making no mention of their meeting, and thus the problem was resolved. The sad aspect of this situation was that the boy trusted a teacher, but would not or could not confide in his own parents.

The school secretary was May Tonn, who had been in the post for several years when Mr Shaw was head. He would meet with her every Monday morning and say, "Let's hear about your weekend, May, and then we can get on..." She was lovely and her motherly advice was sought by pupils and younger teachers alike. Her husband was quite ill and sadly his condition deteriorated so that he could no longer drive their car. At the age of sixty, May learnt to drive, took the test and passed first time.

At the end of the morning assembly the following day, I invited her into the hall and told everyone of her achievement. I then placed a home-made laurel wreath round her neck, which resulted in loud applause, and I gave her a kiss. Of course she was embarrassed, but pleased that the youngsters had expressed not only their congratulations, but their real affection for her as well.

May came with us on an excursion to France where so many things went wrong that I personally had not enjoyed it. I like it when things go like clockwork. As we were returning on the boat, I was feeling rather down, when I came across May sitting on deck looking out to sea. I sat next to her and with real feeling she said, "Oh. Hasn't it been lovely?" I felt ashamed of myself.

During the trip, one of the boys had broken a bottle of perfume which was a present for his mother. Brenda knew the area quite well and walked back to the shop with him to get another one. When I returned to where we were staying, May immediately asked what had happened to Brenda, and when I told her, she was appalled that I had left her. I said, "May, she's a big girl", and they both returned shortly after. But May was disgusted with me!

On one occasion at school, the two of us were chatting, and May asked where Brenda and I were going on holiday that year. I told her my mother was not too well and we might not want to leave her. "I'll look after her for a fortnight", she said immediately.

"You would, too, wouldn't you", I said. Here was May, whose husband needed a great deal of care by then, and yet she would have been prepared to take on my mum, who by that time must have been around eighty years old. I thanked her warmly, but said I couldn't allow her to do it.

The deputy head was Stuart Heath, an imposing presence, who was very keen on sport and discipline, and we had known each other for years. Despite his weight, which he constantly tried to control, he was surprisingly light on his feet, and each year he trained a group to compete in the annual inter-school dancing competition, which Neasden usually won. He made a splendid contribution to out-of-school activities, as did a good number of the staff. I have seen him standing between the field and the playground, refereeing a game of rounders on the field and conducting a cycling proficiency group on the playground, at the same time! He was quite strict, but the pupils appreciated his interest in them and he was well respected.

When Stuart was successful in applying for a headship to another middle school, John Hicks was appointed as his successor. John was not really interested in games, but he made a great contribution when computers were being introduced in the school. I was around fifty years old at that time, and I made the decision that I had managed quite well without them, and if I was spared for another fifty years, the same would apply. This was a bad decision on my part and eventually I tried to learn more, but I have never really become computer friendly.

When he was younger, John was the leader of a scout troop in Anlaby, so we knew each other quite well before he came to Neasden. When I took early retirement, he was appointed head for the remaining five terms, at which point he took early retirement as well. Sadly, he contracted cancer and died shortly after. It must have been one of the shortest retirements on record, but it was good that most of the ex-staff members attended his funeral.

Ann Goforth was senior mistress in all but name (the school had too few pupils to make it a 'special post'), but she was held in great affection by the pupils and staff alike. She had a lovely Scottish accent which I could have listened to for hours, and she was a caring and loyal member of staff. Sadly, she too, died shortly after the middle schools were disbanded.

John Bryan took a very prominent part in the life of the school, and it was he who ran the discos which were very much enjoyed. The disco for the first and second year pupils started more or less immediately after lessons ended, after four o'clock, and the one for the third and fourth years ran later. Several members of staff supported these events, and in the hour between the two discos, one of the staff went out to get meals for us all from the local take-away. I remember that part of the evening with as much pleasure as the discos, since it was a social event in itself.

On the last day of the Christmas term, the pupils were allowed to organise their own entertainment, and our science specialist, Steve Brown, always gave a short excerpt with his guitar. He was very good indeed and I particularly remember his rendering of *Nellie the Elephant* when the entire company joined in the chorus! Some of the contributions made by pupils were splendid. On one occasion, two of the boys performed a turn involving escapology, and even I couldn't see how they did it. There was much dressing up and the act done by four of the fourth-year boys dressed as girls nearly sent me into total hysterics.

I was always keen to let pupils show what talents they had and let them perform in front of the whole school. Any pupil who played an instrument was encouraged to give a recital during an assembly. It was good to see that even the most uninvolved pupils would join in the applause with apparent sincerity. One boy who was an absolute genius with the Rubik cube gave a performance of his skills, another could perform a sort of jerky dance, and he demonstrated this, as well. Another, which I remember, demonstrated his skill by climbing one of the ropes right to the ceiling, using only his hands and arms. One sports day, a boy who was no athlete, came tailing last in one of the long distance races, and got the biggest round of applause of the afternoon for sticking at it right to the end.

Various members of staff ran activities competing in football, cricket, netball, swimming, stamp collecting and other after-school and weekend activities, as well as expeditions. John Gallant organised a skiing trip to Scotland over the Easter break, and other out-of-school projects are mentioned in Chapter 12.

Shortly after I arrived at the school, I was anxious to get the parents more involved, and a 'Parents and Friends Association' was formed. It was good that several of the staff were prepared to help in this way. Over fifteen parents were closely involved and many others were prepared to help with special events. The initial aim for fundraising was to have proper changing rooms and showers, but it very soon became clear that this was much too ambitious an aim. It was then decided that we would work for the school to have its own minibus, and this venture was successful. Norah Spencer, one of the parents, was secretary of the association and her husband, Bev, always organised the archery on many of the outdoor events.

Neasden was one of the only two Junior High Schools in the city to have its own minibus, and the other school was much bigger than ours. It was used for educational visits, excursions, and sports events of all kinds. I made a promise to the pupils that by the end of its first year, every youngster would have one visit of some kind in order to have at least one ride in the minibus. It was used very regularly by those involved with sport, but within a fortnight of the year-end, there were still six pupils who had not had the use of it. A special visit to the old town and Wilberforce House was fixed just for those six pupils.

The Parents and Friends Association bought a minibus for the school.
It was well used!

We used the minibus to take pupils to East Hull Baths and we had the younger son of our member of parliament as a pupil. When he was one of the boys going to the baths, he would take charge at certain points on the route. He was a popular boy and given the fact that East Hull was a strong Labour area, he led the cheering as we passed Labour Headquarters and the booing when we were passing the Conservative Headquarters. The whole operation was conducted in the most civilised way, and when driving the minibus, I was always highly amused by the whole performance.

On one occasion, I had an interchange with the lady who was responsible for art and drama. She accosted me outside the practical block, although I can't remember what it was about. However, I gave the matter some thought and over the lunch break we spoke again. "Did you appreciate, Vera", I said, "that if anyone had been listening to our earlier exchange, they would have had the impression that I was the class teacher and YOU were the head?"

A little conversation followed and we parted in a friendly way. The following day she came into my room, closed the door, and said, "I told my daughter what you said yesterday, and she said to me, 'Mother! I know exactly what he meant!' I just thought I would tell you." Vera had a no nonsense way of speaking and always sounded authoritarian. She was a really good teacher, and if she said 'jump' the pupils all jumped, and quite high as well! But happily, she was also very human.

Sadly, shortly after she retired, she fell backwards down the stairs at home, and was in hospital for a short time. I went to see her several times, but she seemed to have had all the stuffing knocked out of her, and she was very subdued. But again, it was good that many of the staff attended her funeral.

I regarded the morning assembly as the time when there was a real opportunity to establish a good atmosphere, even though there were some occasions when 'the riot act' had to be read. Most of the time the assemblies were enjoyable and I always tried to make them interesting. On one occasion, the theme of the assembly was that if you don't keep alert someone will try to fool you. On the small table in front of me I had six teacups, and I had placed three with their handles to the left and three with their handles to the right.

At this point I had not mentioned what I was leading to, and I asked for a pupil to come up and help. Having chosen one of the first-year boys who were eagerly volunteering, I then began to point out that some of these cups were made for right-handed people and some were for left-handed people. Immediately there was a response from the pupils, some groaning faintly and some amused, but the boy I had chosen was still looking seriously at the cups.

My heart sank when I realised that 'the penny hadn't dropped' with him. I felt almost sick when I thought that he was on the point of being humiliated, but then he looked at me with a grin on his face and said, "Wait a minute!" He had saved himself from being shown up in front of his friends, and I think there would be several others who were still thinking about it when he 'saw the light'.

On another occasion I had a fine specimen of a nettle, which I had planted in an attractive pot placed centre stage at the front. I first told them that when Mrs Brock had seen it in our kitchen on the previous evening, she really thought that the strain of teaching had finally got to me, until I explained why I wanted it. The moral was that weeds are bad, and only good things are cared for. I followed this by comparing it with people – some people are like healthy plants and some are sadly more like weeds.

Yet another assembly was based on a true story and this turned out to have a very marked effect on our lives – Brenda's and mine. We had bought about an acre of land which contained a bomb crater from the war. I gave some details about how it had happened, since I knew the background story about how it came to be there. I then went on to tell them how I was going to clean out the resulting pond and build a series of waterfalls round it. The obvious moral was dropping bombs is bad, but trying to make something nice is good.

At the end of the assembly, and before they all went to their first lesson, Chris Russell and Dave Curtis who were in the fourth year, came to the front and asked if they could come along the following Saturday and help with the job. The entire story of our subsequent friendship would take the space of at least three more chapters, but this happened over thirty years ago, and they are still a big part of our lives!

Staff and their children enjoying themselves in our pool.

As I write this, Brenda and I are on holiday in France. I rang Chris to learn that he is having an unexpected short break in Malta with his wife, Talia. Freya, their daughter, aged eight, is staying with David and his wife Jo and their daughter, Elsie, aged three, in Hull, just down the road from where we live. I then rang Dave to hear that they had all gone to our house to have a dip in the pool with Rob and Vicky's children, Alisha, nine, and Farren, three, who are staying in our house whilst we are away. (I hope you're all following this!)

By the time I rang Rob, they had emerged from the pool and were all playing football on our lawn. I could not possibly have imagined that the story of our bomb hole would lead to a friendship of over thirty years and lead to us having such a great extended family. It has made a very great difference to our lives and we love them all.

Colin Lowther was another pupil who we came to know better, since he had helped in the garden centre from time to time. Later, after he had gone on to the senior high school, his family moved to the Midlands just at the time when he was due to take his GCSEs. He came to stay with us for the necessary six weeks. We thoroughly enjoyed his stay, and later still, when he joined the RAF, he really, REALLY made it clear that he would like me to be there for his passing-out parade, at the end of his basic training. This was one of the two occasions that I 'twagged' (skipped class) as a head teacher. I got lost on my way to his RAF camp, but still managed to be in time to watch his passing-out parade, and to have a pleasant meal with Colin and his parents.

Colin became a dog handler in the RAF, and the next time we saw him was when we returned from holiday, and turned on the television in a routine way. The time was 7.05pm, and there was Colin on the screen, where he was five minutes into a half hour programme giving a presentation of his experiences as a dog handler, complete with his dog. He was brilliant! When I had suggested to him that we should keep in touch, he excused himself by saying, "I'm not much of a letter writer." If he should happen to read this we would be delighted for him to make contact again, even after all this time.

I mentioned earlier that I can usually see the funny side of many situations, and I have seldom regretted being able to do this. On one occasion, I encountered Nick, our Head of English, in the entrance to the practical block, just after the bell had gone for the lunch break. The division wall to the right of the entrance was about eight feet high leaving a gap at the top, with the cookery area at the other side. The cookery teacher was in the habit of reprimanding girls at eighty decibels. (She shouted a lot!)

Nick had arrived at the entrance in the closing seconds of one such reprimand, which had ended with the words, "ARE YOU DEAF?" The girl had answered in a very subdued voice, "I am now, Miss!"

Nick was absolutely helpless with laughter as I arrived, and he appeared to be engaged with an exercise in trying to swallow his handkerchief. We both went through the left door and closed it. When he had regained his composure, he told me what he had heard, by which time the cookery teacher and the girl had left for lunch. We were then able to return to the main building without embarrassment.

One lunchtime, two girls arrived back at school totally drunk! (Comment from the audience: "He's making it up, now!" Answer: "No. I assure you it's true!")

They were brought to my room and I was dealing with them, when there was a knock on my door, and in walked John Bryan who was their form teacher. They were pleasant girls and he couldn't understand why I was remonstrating with them so strongly. I mouthed to him the information that they were drunk. He was totally amazed, but within about ten seconds he appreciated the situation.

It appeared that at one of the girl's homes there was a drinks cupboard and the pair of them had been sampling a good selection of the contents. Luckily, the other girl's mother was at home, and they were both escorted there so that Mum took charge of them for the afternoon. The following morning the mother of the girl who owned the drinks cupboard came in to see me. She was embarrassed and upset, and said, "Whatever must you think of us?"

There would have been no point in 'piling on the agony', and I played the whole incident light heartedly. They had been experimenting, they had learnt their lesson, they were very upset, and I was sure it would never happen again. I reassured her that however nice a child is, they sometimes let themselves down. She was really relieved; we talked for a while, and parted in a friendly way.

On another occasion, two fourth-year girls came to my room bringing with them an old lady they had found wandering about in the snow and very clearly cold and confused. My first thought was, "They bring me lost dogs, small birds, lost property and now it's old ladies!" However, I felt very proud that they had taken the initiative to help her. After she had been sitting in my room by the fire for a while and had a cup of tea, she was able to tell us roughly where she lived. When we took her in the general area where they had found her, her daughter came up to claim her, and she too was very pleased that the girls had bothered to help.

Around this time, a friend of mine had acquired twelve turkey chicks. Apparently he worked near a place where turkey eggs were incubated on a commercial basis, and they took the view that any eggs which had not hatched on time were probably infertile. These eggs were put on a rubbish heap, and he found that twelve chicks had, in fact, hatched rather late. He knew of my interest in hatching chickens' eggs and gave them to me. Unfortunately, six of them died almost immediately, but the remaining chicks started to thrive.

I took them to school, which created much interest and they became quite tame. I looked after them at home at weekends and at holiday time, but when we went away for a holiday ourselves, one of the mothers was keen to take them home and care for them. The pupils followed their progress with great interest, but the time came when they grew so big that even taking one bird to school was quite an exercise, so I kept them at Evergreens. When I was weeding the garden, they would follow me around and by this time, they were very tame indeed.

One Saturday, Brenda and I were having lunch when the phone rang. It was Maria from next door who said, "I don't want to worry you, Phil, but your turkeys are just making their way across our field on their way to Hull." (We lived just outside the city boundary.) I ran out and they were so tame that all I had to do was to shout, "Hey! Where do you think YOU'RE all going; get back here AT ONCE!" They obeyed straight away and despite the fact that we had no boundary fence there at that time, they never strayed again. They would follow me round when I was weeding in the Christmas trees (we had about 2,000 trees all at different stages of growth). The first time Rusty (our neighbour's dog on the other side) saw them, he barked at them furiously. However, they all turned on him and chased him right up to our neighbour's back door!

Eventually, Christmas was approaching and the project had always been a joint venture with the school. The time approached when they had to be 'prepared for the table'. I then had a call from some agency or other asking me how I was going to kill them. I had hoped I would have the courage to do this myself, since I had dealt with many of our chickens in this way. However, I was informed that this was against the law and they had to be dealt with by an approved company. At first, I thought that it was one of my 'friends' pulling my leg, but it seemed that turkeys come under the same regulations as larger animals and birds and have to be killed in an abattoir.

I found the necessary telephone number, and when I explained that this was a project connected with the school, they agreed to do the job for us free of charge. When I took them to the abattoir, I shall take to my grave the reproachful looks which I got from them! I'm sure they KNEW!

Four of them were sold for school funds, one was the raffle prize for the Christmas Fayre, and Brenda and I had one for Christmas, in exchange for the work and cash we had given to the project, mainly by feeding them. The spin-off was that the pupils realised, some for the first time, that not all animals and birds are pets, but are produced to provide us with food. This was the reason why we never gave them names.

Pupils in high spirits at an inter-school football match.

I was always struck by the difference in the way pupils matured during their passage through the school. At nine years of age, they are definitely still children, but at thirteen some are still children, while others are well on their way to being young adults. I think that children mature to the degree that their parents allow them to mature.

On one occasion, the grandma of a twelve-year-old pupil came to see me. She was quite voluble about the fact that her grandson was being bullied at school. For a while, I couldn't get a word in at all, but after about five minutes, I was able to say something. "Can we go back a bit", I said, "to what you were saying, about when you were bathing him you noticed bruises? You were bathing him?"

She retreated immediately, saying, "Well I just looked in to see how he was getting on." I felt very strongly that her first statement had been more accurate.

The boy was immature and, sadly, this is one reason for children sometimes being bullied.

By way of contrast, a man who arrived one day with his two sons, Sanjay and Anjay, turned out to be a doctor who had just arrived in our area, and the family were from abroad. He wanted to register them into the school and his instructions to me were, "I want them to work hard, and if they do not work hard you will, please, thrash them!" He was a really pleasant man and concerned about his boys, and within a very short time we discovered that:

(a) the boys were very sensible and grown up;

(b) they were lovely lads; and

(c) they were very friendly and popular with everyone.

I could no more have imagined laying a finger on them than I would have considered throwing myself under a bus!

On one occasion, I was invited to spend a day with a Hull manufacturing firm in connection with the idea of schools being linked with industry. I was escorted round for the whole day, and at midday I was invited to have lunch in the executive dining room. I enjoyed a really good meal preceded by a drink at the bar, and followed by coffee. I asked my escort quietly whom I should see regarding payment and he looked at me in total amazement, assuring me that the meal was regarded by his firm as hospitality, and payment was out of the question.

In contrast, I attended a full-day head teachers' meeting at the education centre (an old school which had been converted, but not much!) Towards the end of the meal – a basic salad followed by a basic dessert – the Senior Inspector circulated round the tables collecting sixty pence from each of us to cover the cost of the meal. Now I am not in favour of money for education being squandered, but I regarded the exercise as being rather humiliating for a man in his position. Full-day meetings of head teachers were quite rare and I would have thought that the cost of the meal could have been covered somehow.

Half-day meetings of head teachers were held on a regular basis, and most of them were quite valuable, but one which I attended was totally awful. I cannot remember the exact details, but on the following day, I had a phone call from one of the inspectors who had been present. After he had assured me that he wanted an honest answer, I told him that in my opinion it had been a complete waste of time and that the speaker was useless. Apparently that was the opinion of everyone whom he had contacted. I was never very keen of being out of school during the day; I was paid for doing a job, and I was being taken away from it, but to have a half day utterly wasted in this way was appalling.

When I found out that all the middle schools would be closing within two years, I rather lost heart. The middle schools formed an excellent 'bridge' between primary schools and the high schools, and enabled pupils to be introduced to specialist teaching gradually, over four years. I really believed in the system and as the closing of the middle schools was linked with sixth form colleges being introduced, it would have been far too expensive for the four stages to operate at the same time. In addition, the birth rate had been falling, so that many middle schools were feeling the pinch. The most dramatic example of this was one such school which could take six hundred pupils, had dropped to below one hundred.

The local authority had guaranteed that all middle schools would have nine specialist teachers, which made many of them very expensive to run. I must point out that while the pupil numbers had been dropping in nearly all the middle schools for the previous five or six years, our numbers had increased from about two-hundred and seventy to almost three-hundred and fifty. And this was in a catchment area where practically no extra houses were being built. We must have been doing something right!

I applied for early retirement, and I was really pleased that the Assistant Chief Inspector visited me one afternoon trying to persuade me to carry on. I really appreciated that, and it was certainly better than being given the impression that they would be glad to be seeing the back of me.

I was overwhelmed by the events of my last week at Neasden. The Parents and Friends Association threw a party for Brenda and me on the Saturday evening before I was due to leave. When Bas Dale spoke at the party, reference was made to our camps and at one point he said, "If you want five star cooking in the middle of a field, he's your man", pointing in my direction. This had to be a slight exaggeration, but on three occasions I was asked by the local inspector involved with outdoor pursuits, to cater on the one-week course for teachers who were going to be involved with running one of the Farndale camps, so I can't be too bad a cook!

I would really rather have been remembered for some things more educational, like being involved in the early stages when the Nuffield Science Scheme was introduced, and helping to run in-service courses for younger teachers within the authority. However, the evening was very light-hearted and I was pleased that the event had been mooted and that so many people had turned up. Nick Dyson, who was our Head of English, filmed all the events in my final week at Neasden, including the party, the carol concert and much more. I saw all the films right through quite recently and it was really good to remember it all.

Tailpiece: It is now twenty-two years since the middle schools closed and there has been an Ex-Neasden JHS Staff Christmas Dinner every year since then. I have no hand in making the arrangements, but I get invited, and it is really, really good to feel welcome on these occasions, and to meet everyone again. One of the sad aspects of growing old is attending the funerals of friends, many of whom I have known for years, and, sadly, a good number of my ex-colleagues have now died. The events of my last week at Neasden brought home to me how much I would miss it all. However, life goes on, and there were very many other things I wanted to do before the 'great reaper' took over. I'm reminded of the saying, 'It isn't what you've done that saddens you – it's what you haven't done'. And we still had a LOT of things we wanted to do!

CHAPTER 10
Links With The Scout Association

From a very early age I had always wanted to be 'in scouts' but the scout group at Market Weighton had been disbanded at the outbreak of war. However, in 1944, a new vicar was appointed to All Saints Church – Rev. J. Massingherd-Mundy. He had led a scout troop in the past, and he re-started the scouts at Market Weighton. I couldn't wait to join, and before we left the town to come back to Hull, I had achieved my Second Class Badge.

After we returned to Hull, a friend of mine at school told me that he was in the Portobello (Methodist) Scout Group, and in the September I went along there. It turned out to be a large group which had kept running throughout the war years, and for Mr Robert Bellwood, it was his life. The group had a drum and fife band which maintained a high standard for many years. I became totally involved and integrated in the group, and what I did not appreciate until a good few years later, was how many real friendships would be forged which have been maintained for my entire life. Round about 1950, Mr Bellwood managed to secure a piece of land quite near the church where the group was affiliated. It was owned by a local firm, and had been intended as a building site for a pair of semi-detached houses, but on the understanding that a scout headquarters would be built there, the group was able to buy it for a token one hundred pounds.

It was several years before enough money was saved and even then it could not have been considered without most of the work being done on a voluntary basis. The group had a very strong Parents and Friends Association with over twenty members and as a result of their efforts with fund raising, and by the efforts of the scouts, we were eventually able to make a start. The Group Scout Leader insisted that no work would be done on Sundays, but every Saturday and weeknights in the summer, work was in progress. One Saturday afternoon, a scout was given the job of 'brewing-up' for everyone. He counted the number of boys and adults on the site and on the calculation of one teaspoonful of tea for every person, plus one 'for the pot', he put twenty-seven spoonfuls of tea in the teapot. Once several of us had tasted the result, there were very few takers for the tea break on that particular day.

Building the headquarters took four years, and for about six or eight of us, it almost took over our lives. Ron Lawson had been in the group longer than I had, and he agreed to take charge of the building work. Ron was a time-served electrician, but over the years he had kept his eyes open on a whole range of building sites and learnt a lot about the skills needed, apart from electrical work. He did the work voluntarily, like the rest of us, and when the headquarters was completed, he has continued working on maintenance and upkeep. Ron's father also worked really hard at the job, and John Raddings, who was a Humber Pilot, often worked on the site on his own, when the rest of us were at work or school. One day, he slipped and fell into one of the drainage trenches which were full of rainwater. Soaking wet, he jumped on his bike, went home, donned dry clothes, cycled back to the site and completed the painting of one of the window frames.

I had always fancied myself at bricklaying, but on my first day, when I had taken nearly two hours to lay fourteen bricks, I began to understand that I still had a lot to learn. However, I speeded up in time and, along and with a good number of others, I managed to lay several thousand bricks. However, I would never have been able to make my living at it.

After the roof of the building was completed, we were all in the same position regarding the plastering; none of us felt able to tackle it and we couldn't afford to have it done for us. It was at this stage that an ex-scout from the group, Arthur Read, who by that time was a well-respected businessman, came along and said that he would be prepared to pay for the plastering to be done professionally. Several years before, he had bought a trek cart for the group, in memory of his brother, who had been killed during the Second World War. As a result, the whole building was plastered in under a month.

As work progressed, we were surprised to find that in one area of the site there was a circle, about six feet across, which was a different colour from the rest of the surrounding clay. In fact, it was soil. We dug down to about five feet with soil and hard core still being removed and our theory was that at one time this had been a well. We then threw the soil back, along with more hard core and brought it back to the right level again.

All the scouts, even the younger ones, worked on the site, and it became an excellent example of how dedicated youngsters can be when older ones are totally committed.

We were able to have the official opening of the headquarters on 7th April

1962, and the place was packed. Lord Middleton had kindly agreed to perform the opening ceremony, and the entire afternoon was thoroughly enjoyed by all. At this stage, three of us had leant the group twenty pounds each, to keep the accounts 'in the black' and I even had to pay for two brass hooks to hold the main doors open as people filed in. During the following week, we had some activity organised for each evening, so that many more people could see our efforts.

Work on the scout headquarters. (Drawing by Stuart Moor – ex-scouter of the group.)

We must include a word or two of warning for any scout group considering building their own headquarters. On one occasion, I was on my own, taking down some scaffolding and when one of the clamps was being unfastened, the entire framework collapsed. If anyone had been in the area they could well have been killed. Similarly, one scout fell off the edge of some scaffolding, and again, this could have been serious. One boy walked straight into the end of a scaffolding pole and his eye could have been badly damaged. Finally, it is essential that one competent person volunteers to be in charge. There aren't that many Ron Lawsons about!

Four years later, the extra accommodation was completed, but by this time, we had been able to afford for the bricklaying and the plastering to be done professionally. The opening ceremony was performed by Sir Len Hutton, on 29th January, 1966. The rear hall has a ceiling made up of fifteen large leaf outlines cut out in three bays of five, so that the fluorescent lights shine through the leaves. These are actual enlarged tree leaf outlines, and represent one of the contributions which I made to the building.

Portobello (Methodist) Scout Group, c. 1960.

We have been very lucky at Portobello that a good number of old scouts have been ready to help the group in some way. Johnny Thirlwell agreed to take charge of the memorabilia room, and has spent hundreds of man-hours gathering together photographs, log books, badges, stories and so on. In addition to the work he has done at home, he spends every Tuesday morning working at the headquarters. The collection causes great interest for visitors, not least on the anniversary afternoon, when about eighty old scouts, on average, gather together, usually on the second Saturday in November.

A new sign for the headquarters.

In 2005, we had the premises valued so that we were properly covered for insurance purposes, and the combined value of the building and the site was over half a million pounds. As I write this in 2013, I am still in contact with well over fifty friends who have been, and some still are, members of the group and a good proportion meet together socially on a regular basis. Sadly, a number have now died and several others are living abroad but we still exchange news and cards at Christmas.

* * * * * * * * * * * * * * * * * * *

During the Second World War, despite the shortages and restrictions, all the usual activities were continued, although many of the adult leaders were 'called up'. The annual camp took place every year at Levisham, a small village in the North Yorkshire Moors, on land administered by the Stationmaster. The group was able to send the camping equipment ahead by rail, and the members, too, went by rail, arriving at Levisham right next to where the camp was to be set up. My first camp was after the war ended, and I still remember the strange shapes which had been painted on the tents as camouflage from enemy aircraft.

Hull sustained much bomb damage, but weekend camps were held right through the war just outside the city, at Wawne. Many scout meetings were interrupted by the siren sounding so that refuge had to be sought in the air-raid shelter. One of the many log books written at the time mentioned this happening, and how one man let it be known that the scouts should be outside helping. He set a good example by staying in the shelter until the 'all clear' was sounded!

Mr Bellwood, the skipper, serviced all the band instruments and kept the whole group and the band going right through the war and beyond. He never married, and all his free time was involved with his church membership and running the scout group. When he was older, he had many problems with his health so that eventually he had to abandon camping altogether, and finally give up running the group. Thus it was that when I was still in my twenties, as scoutmaster (later known as scout leader), I was in charge of running many of the activities including the annual camp with as many as forty or more of us under canvas.

* * * * * * * * * * * * * * * * * * *

I was always afraid of being typecast as a teacher, and when on holiday or away from home, I never let it be known, since most people can remember at least one teacher they absolutely hated, or worse still, despised. It was towards the end of one of our camps that I went over to the farmhouse to settle the camp fee with the farmer. In the course of the conversation, he said to me, "What does tha' do for a living?" I had to admit that I was a school teacher, and his reply of, "Yis, I thawt tha' was!" really shattered me. I pondered on what there was about me that would lead him to this conclusion. When I go on holiday meeting new people, I never let it be known that I am a teacher, since some people have impressions from their youth that teachers are a race apart!

I had been quite lucky being introduced into a scout group which had been well led for so very long, but when anyone takes up the reins of being the leader of such a group, the challenge of keeping up the reputation is immense.

Most of the scout leaders were known by their first names, but in the case of Mr Bellwood he was always known as 'skipper' or 'skip' which is the norm in many scout groups. It never occurred to any of us to call him by his first name. He had held the position for so long, and was so very much older, it would have seemed very strange for me to take over the title. I was always 'Phil' to the boys, but if anyone in the school addressed me in that way, I would consider it to be most inappropriate. As far as the respect was concerned, the relationship was totally different, and 'sir' was always the norm at school. However, on one occasion in the laboratory, a boy had become so involved with his experiment that he called to me, "Hey, Dad, come and look at this." He was immediately embarrassed and apologised, but I felt pleased that the mistake had been made and that he was so excited about something he was doing. On one occasion, I found myself saying to a class, "Don't get so excited", when they were really interested about some experiment. It was only later I reflected on the fact that this was exactly how I wanted them to be affected by the work.

Back with the scouts, we were lucky enough to be able to store our equipment and run activities at a farm about a mile away from the headquarters. The farmer, Mr Wright, had four sons who were all grown up, but every one of them had been scouts in the group. Mr Wright had served in the carnage of the First World War and had lost a leg in the fighting. He was fairly gruff in manner, but as far as he was concerned, the scouts could do no wrong. We were able to use his farm for all sorts of pioneering projects, including building rope bridges of all kinds, rafts and aerial runways and during the summer we were there on many Saturday afternoons. This, of course, was before our time became preoccupied for four years with building the headquarters.

Once I had returned to Hull after my army service and college, I was keen to be fully trained as an adult scout leader, and this involved a written course and practical work on a series of weekends or a full week's course at the International Training Centre at Gilwell Park in Essex. I opted to go to Gilwell Park, and never regretted that decision, because it opened my eyes to the wider aspect of the movement. Not long after this, I was asked to be on the staff of the Adult Leader Training Team in the county and later, I eventually served five years as the leader of the team.

The scout county did not have a headquarters when I became involved. We finally managed to buy about six acres of land at Raywell, where the buildings had been a TB sanatorium, with open verandas at the front. When the building was renovated, there was accommodation for twenty-four people, plus a kitchen, dining area, and toilets. The final stage of improvement was when four activity rooms were added at the rear, and the opening was performed by the Duchess of Kent.

In about 1972, Brenda won an award from the bank and she was able to choose to go anywhere in the world for a month, with the condition that there was a project involved with the visit. For her project Brenda chose to find out more about the Scout Association in America, with particular reference to Leader Training. All her expenses were paid and about half of mine, and we were both to be involved in the project. The complete visit would easily take up three chapters, but we were both treated to fantastic hospitality and our whole visit was arranged by Scout Headquarters in London and the American Scout Headquarters.

Initially, we had two days in New York and then went on to Washington and from there to various places along the east coast as far as Miami. When we looked out of the window at our hotel, I could see the swimming pool which looked very inviting. Brenda flopped on the bed, but I went out to the pool, and I was there for no more than ten minutes. The following day my back was bright red. (Warning to others – the sun there is almost directly overhead!)

Our next stop was New Orleans and eventually back to New York, en route for home. Originally, we had arranged to travel by train, but we were assured by officials in New York that this would exhaust us, so they changed the programme allowing us to cover the longer distances by air.

Everywhere we went, we experienced warmth and friendship and the hospitality was superb. We had experienced the fellowship of scouting in the UK, but our eyes were opened to the worldwide aspect of scouting.

In 1965, a County Camp was held at Burton Constable when the Chief Scout, Sir Charles McClean, visited. There were two thousand scouts in camp and on the Saturday afternoon, two thousand cub scouts visited the camp. Eric Martin and I are great friends, and when he was put in charge of the entire organisation, he chose me as his deputy. This was a very rewarding experience but it meant that if he was ill or otherwise afflicted, the whole responsibility would have fallen on me. Happily, he remained fit throughout the camp. There were many meetings in the six months leading up to the camp, so that everyone knew what was happening and what was expected. We had about fifty senior scouts helping with the organisation, and they were very impressive. There was no mains water on the site, and during the camp they kept up a shuttle service bringing fresh water from Sproatley village, about a mile and a half away, using several huge tanks with trailers and tractors. On the Saturday evening, the last journey was just arriving at half past ten o'clock, as I was going to bed.

The older scouts also built a rope suspension bridge during the weekend which created much interest. To illustrate its strength, they pushed a small car over it. Brian Skelton, from Portobello Group set up a telephone system between all the sub-camps and the administration tent, and this was well used.

Brenda and I financed the building of a cabin for handicapped scouts (now called extension scouts), and I helped a great deal with the actual building. It can be used by other scouts for weekends and, although there was no plaque on it, our intention was that this was in memory of our parents. At that time I did quite a bit of work at Raywell, and it was actually my suggestion when we first bought the property, that it should be called Raywell Park. I also built a 'castle' for youngsters to play in, but later it had to be destroyed to make way for a toilet block. I built the open-air chapel for Scouts' Own Services, and served for several years on the committee which administered the site.

On several occasions, I went along to Gilwell Park to help with one of the Wood Badge courses for adults. There was a brass reproduction of Baden-Powell's footprint on the site, and in the store were five more such reproductions. I was instrumental in getting one of these footprints for Raywell Park on the understanding that it was regarded as being 'on loan'. I also built the small base on which it was displayed, along with a plaque explaining its origin.

Brenda served with Willerby Carr Lane Cub Scout Pack as leader for many years, and was later the Assistant District Commissioner for Cub Scouts in Haltemprice.

After I relinquished my responsibility with the Leader Training Team, I served as Assistant County Commissioner for the Scout Fellowship, which I held for five years. This was the last warrant I held and I also gave up my warrant as Group Scout Leader at Portobello. Brenda and I are now both Vice Presidents in the Scout County, which is an honorary position, but in a way acknowledges the contribution we have made to scouting over the years. I still have my interest at Portobello, serving as the Chairman of the Group Council, and getting involved with other jobs from time to time.

Even before the group had bought the land for the headquarters, it had always been hoped that it would be done at some point. This really helped in recruiting parents and friends for the supporters committee, and we had about twenty adults involved. At one point, the money raised was barely keeping up with the way that building materials were increasing in price. All those involved, scouts and adults, worked very hard to raise funds, collecting jam jars and waste paper, having jumble sales and a range of other money-raising events. When I was younger, one of the first chairmen of the committee was Harold Duncan, who served for very many years. He was succeeded by Ron Dale and they both gave sterling service, both before the headquarters was built and afterwards.

Preparing a 3-course meal at Raywell Park for over 100 diners.

I have mentioned before that we are lucky to have so many friends who were scouts at Portobello, when I was younger. Some we see very regularly and others are in contact fairly infrequently, but we always exchange cards and news in the run-up to Christmas. Robert Hatfield, who has spent his entire married life in Canada, still comes to Hull regularly to see his mum. He it was, who proof read the first chapter of this book, since this sort of exercise had been involved with his job. He spent two-and-a-half hours with me, and his advice was invaluable.

Nearer to home, and once the headquarters was in full use, we used to end the meetings with a 'canteen'. For many years, 'Mrs Mac', the mother of two of the scouts, Jim, and later, Paul Mackinder, ran this facility, and later, it was taken over by Bunty Mann. I became great friends with the Mackinder family, and before he had his own motorbike, Jim would ride pillion with me. At one stage, when I was a late teenager, and later, there were about eight of us with five bikes between us, and although we rode about all over the place, we NEVER had an accident.

John Phillips and his wife Joan are lucky enough to have a house in Garden Village – the first one ever built, actually – and John has given great support helping me to sort out our personal finances. Brenda always did this work, but lately her memory is rather faulty, and I am totally ignorant regarding most financial matters. Vaughan Smith and his wife, Linda, have lived at Scarborough for years, and we always have a meal out with them, when we spend a few days staying overlooking the North Bay. Many others live further afield and we only see them infrequently, but the links are still there.

Charles and Mary Laing are regular contacts, and it was Charles who rode pillion with me down to the camp organised for the troop in Brentford, when I was at college all those years ago. We alternate with them and Glyn Webster and his wife Annette, having a meal quite regularly on a random basis. Glyn and I were colleagues when we were both on the staff at East Mount County HS. When he was getting married, our present to them was to paper their living room.

Phil Woodford and his wife, Irene, have lived on the Isle of Man for most of their married life. Several of us motored to their wedding on the other side of the Pennines, and in the evening we toured the Blackpool Illuminations. We 'topped off' the day by getting lost on the way home and ending in a farmyard near Sherburn-in-Elmet! This was before the M62 was made.

Roger King and his wife have spent most of their married life in Australia, and he is now Professor King. When he was young, it was generally acknowledged that he had more brains than any four of us put together, but he integrated well into the group, and was very popular. He spent some of his spare time at one summer camp reading the whole of *War and Peace*, and he now has so many letters after his name that he has had to increase the size of his visiting card!

George Dennis was always quite a character and he stayed in the group, when older, as an adult leader. While in the army, he joined the Catterick Rovers, and this year he has been attending their fifty-third annual reunion. Sadly, his wife, Loreli has suffered with her health and is now in a nursing home, but he goes to see her every single day.

Adrian Mann is another old scout who stayed on in the group as an adult leader. His mum was on the Parents and Friends Association, and she took a major part, over several years, helping with the Christmas Day parties, which we ran for over thirty years. These were run for any older people who would otherwise be on their own on Christmas Day. Adrian did a lot of work as an adult leader, until he moved with his family to Stockton-on-Tees.

Over the years, a number of old scouts stayed on to be adult leaders, and Portobello were really fortunate in this way. The complete list would fill several paragraphs, but mention should be made of the Moor family. Stuart Moor was an assistant leader for some time. Although he was rather quiet, he was far more popular than he ever realised, and his parents and auntie gave much good service with the Supporters Association.

At the present time, Portobello is lucky to have a number of younger leaders who make a good contribution to the running of the group. Keith Pickering has been the Group Scout Leader for several years now, with his wife, Jo, running the Beavers. John and Elaine Prosser are staunch supporters, with John as the Assistant Group Scout Leader. Andy Marrit leads the Explorer Scouts, Lee Sims is the Scout Leader, with Alex Norman as his assistant. Dan Appleby is the Cub Scout Leader while Jo Wallis is Assistant Cub Scout Leader. Along with several other younger people, they form a strong team.

Many people will remember the Lyke Wake Walk, forty-two miles of hiking from Osmotherly to Ravenscar, over very rough moorland in North Yorkshire. For several years, Portobello Group organised this event on a large scale, and usually over a hundred took part. Sadly, organised groups are now discouraged from doing it, because the moorland was being worn away.

Once, when I had been on the support team, yet again, someone asked me how many times I had actually completed the walk myself. I was sorry to report that I had never done it, and those involved stated that, quite definitely, I would be one of the walkers the following year. For the first thirty miles, I really enjoyed it, but the last twelve were a real slog. However, my time was just under fifteen hours.

On one occasion, Ken and Doreen Brook completed the walk, and I encountered them slumped against a wall at the end of their achievement. Both of them looked shattered, and Ken looked at me and said, "I'm going to the doctor on Monday morning", and then there was a pause. "I'm going to get my bloody head examined", he said.

Their son, Chris, was also a scout, and when his father sadly died, it was he who wanted Doreen to present me with his fine walking stick, which has a compass in the top. This has always had pride of place in our living room, along with a poem, which Doreen also passed on to me.

Leslie and Amy Boot were also strong supporters of the group. For years, Leslie audited all the group accounts, and they were both keen workers in many other ways. Their son, Robin, was another of the many older scouts who stayed on to give service as an adult leader.

Rob Armstrong and Betty go back a long way in the history of the group, for it was Rob who started the Rover Crew round about the time when the headquarters was built. He it was who put forward the idea of having the Christmas Day party, for older people who would otherwise have been entirely on their own. The Rover Crew visited seventy or eighty old people who would be eligible, and it was really pleasing to find that a high proportion of those visited had been invited by friends, neighbours and relatives to spend the day with them. However, there were fifteen people who would otherwise have been on their own, and they formed the basis for that first year. The rear hall was transformed for the day, with fireplace, carpet, easy chairs, piano, and, of course, a television. Cars were laid on to collect them at about eleven o'clock, the Christmas dinner was at twelve-thirty and the afternoon programme included games, the Queen's speech, carols and the visit of Father Christmas with a gift for all the visitors. After a salad tea, cars took the guests back home, along with a good few items left from the catering, to be eaten on Boxing Day.

It all became an annual event, with the number of guests never being fewer than about twenty-four, and on occasions being over thirty. The main 'workers' over the years included Margaret Williams and Arthur, Bunty Mann and Adrian, the Armstrong family, the Jowitt family, the Finch family, the Brewer family,

Eileen Walker and Roy and many others. My own contribution was to cook the Christmas dinner, but there were many other helpers. In the end, as a result of more sheltered accommodation and care homes being opened, the party became unnecessary, but it had served to make great Christmases for many, many people.

Tailpiece: The headquarters has now been open for nearly forty years, and a great deal of time has been spent on upkeep and maintenance, led by Ron Lawson. Frank Coxall also spent many hours working and cleaning to keep everything shipshape, before, sadly, he died. He had been a scout at Portobello well before the war and, after he retired, he spent much time keeping the headquarters spick and span. We're very lucky to have so many friends with a feeling for the place. As I write this, the group is celebrating its ninetieth anniversary, having been operating continuously since 1923.

CHAPTER 11
Rob And The Garden Centre

If it had not been for Rob coming to Evergreens, much of the development work would never have even been tackled, never mind completed. Brenda and I never aimed to have a big garden centre and even now it is nowhere near as huge as the 'supermarket' garden centres which have developed all over the country.

We first met Rob by chance. One night, Brenda and I had gone out for the evening and we made a call at a house quite near to where he lived. I happened to drop my cheque book, and the following day I had a call from the lady whose son had found it. I shot round to the house to thank him and leave a small financial thank you for him. I also told his mum that we had a swimming pool adjoining our house. If he wanted to pop round for a dip with a few of his friends, they would be very welcome. Two days later her son Martin Spencer came around with Rob, his brother Geoff, and Wayne Ede, who lived nearby. They all went in the pool and later Paul Dixon and Rob's other brother Ben started coming, usually four or five at a time. Rob and Wayne actually came with me one weekend to visit Chris on his yacht near Ipswich. We were able to do all this because, at that time, the garden centre was only just starting up. They visited the pool quite regularly that summer and several succeeding summers and we are still friends with all of them.

When he was thirteen, Rob became a weekend boy in the nursery so that we got to know him rather better, and when he left school we asked him if he would want to work full time with us. Before he started, we made sure his parents were in agreement as well. During the first two years, he was in the nursery for four days a week, and attended the College of Agriculture for one day a week. As a result of this, he gained his Level 2 NVQ in Horticulture.

A different tutor from the college visited him at Evergreens each term, and on one occasion, we all received a 'pat on the back'. The lady concerned spoke to Rob for some time as he gave her a tour of the place and then she came to us for coffee. "I've told him he's very lucky to have found you two", she said, "and now I'm telling you, YOU'RE very lucky to have found HIM!"

Rob's full name is Robert Whitehouse Smith, the middle part being Rob's grandfather's middle name. This has now been handed on to Vicky and Rob's son – Farren Whitehouse Smith.

During Rob's first year, we decided that it would be good if we had a three-day visit to another garden centre outside our immediate area, and we both really enjoyed the experience. We went in the *caravette* and, apart from us enjoying it, I felt that it was good experience for us both. We decided that the following year we would visit another place and, to cut a long story short, we visited ten different places during his first ten years. We visited the Chelsea Flower Show, a large conifer nursery, a nursery in Wales, and we even went to the Eden Project and the Lost Gardens of Heligan. On one occasion, Chris was home, so the three of us went together and on the last morning we were on a campsite that provided breakfasts. Bacon and egg and all the extras really set us up for the day.

The first two projects which Rob tackled went really well, and the first big job which we tackled together was raising the roof of the piggery building. The side walls were only four feet high and the building was twenty feet wide and fifty feet long, and we raised the roof by two feet. Without going into detail, this was quite a long job, and we discovered that we worked really well together.

Now, over twenty years later, we still work well together, the only difference being that Rob has become the main man, and I am definitely the assistant. I am writing this chapter after my eightieth birthday, and I am not just semi-retired, but almost completely retired. I do much less of the heavy work, and since Rob became the manager over ten years ago he is running the place, and doing it very well indeed. However, like all small businesses just now, in 2013, we are feeling the effect of the recession and we're 'hanging in there'.

When we had been operating for three or four years as Evergreens Nursery we were offered the chance from the local authority to have advice about running the place. We took them up on this, and the lady who arrived was absolutely brilliant. Although she was with us for only half a day her advice was invaluable. Almost her first words were, "What are you doing calling yourselves a nursery? You're not a nursery, you're a garden centre!"

By that time, we had developed somewhat, but we had hesitated in calling ourselves a garden centre, thinking we might be regarded as arrogant. However, she reeled off a number of things which we were dealing with by that time and insisted we were a garden centre, so that's what we became. Many of the garden centres these days are more like supermarkets, and we often get the comment made that we are a real garden centre. I think by this people mean we don't sell clothing, furniture, groceries, and such like, but concentrate mainly on items for the garden, particularly plants and shrubs. In addition, we always try to greet visitors individually.

Tristan has worked here part time for fourteen years now, and he is very conscientious indeed, as well as being very knowledgeable in giving advice to customers. Two years ago, Jodie presented him with a son, Spencer, and within the last two months he has been in the pool. He's not too sure about me yet, but I feel that next year, he'll be swimming, even if it is a struggle. Whenever Brenda and I visit other garden centres, we're quite surprised how difficult it is sometimes to find anyone who has the time and the knowledge to give advice. We try to make ourselves as available as possible and make people feel welcome. One other thing that customers remark about is how friendly we are, not only to them, but with each other. We're very lucky to have such a good little team.

Spencer, Tristan and Jodie.

The name of 'Vicky' seemed to be coming up in Rob's conversation more and more so that eventually they became 'an item', and soon after that, she was working part time at the garden centre. It was three months later when Vicky said in conversation to me, "Well you used to know my granddad." Her surname was Moon, and almost in disbelief I said, "You're Fred Moon's granddaughter?" Her grandad and I had both been involved in the scout movement in East Hull District, before Vicky had even been born, and, for me, it had taken all that time before the penny dropped.

Vicky became more and more involved with the garden centre and Vicky and Rob became more and more involved with each other, and in 1999 they were married. St. Peter's Church, in Bilton was full, and everyone, not least me, were really sorry that Rob's next brother, Geoff, was unable to be the best man, as planned. The evening before, he had cut his arm very badly indeed and was in hospital, having lost quite a bit of blood. However, Paul Dixon filled the bill, even though the suit didn't fit too well! The wedding photographs, of course, were taken in the garden at Evergreens.

Me, Alisha, Farren and Rob in our pool.

Immediately after the wedding, Brenda and I went to see Geoff in hospital, and he looked really awful. It may have cheered him up a bit to see us, but it certainly didn't cheer us up! However, by the Wednesday, he looked a good deal better. The real downside was that some of the nerves in his arm had been damaged, and he had lost the feeling in two of his fingers. Over the years, Geoff had done a lot of work at Evergreens and we felt very sad for him, but within a few months, the feeling in his arm and fingers had returned.

Four years later Vicky presented Rob with a baby daughter, Alisha May, and Vicky's involvement with the garden centre had to take a back seat for a short while. Alisha is now nine years old, and she's lovely. Vicky had always been very skilled with flowers and floristry, and having completed a course at the College of Agriculture she has the qualification of Level 2 NPTC Diploma in Floristry – with distinction. She is rapidly building up a name for herself supplying flowers for weddings, funerals and bouquets for all occasions.

When Alisha was five, Brenda and I really hoped that there would be another little Smith before long, and they knew this. When the four of us went on a day visit to London, Vicky waited until we were right at the top of the Millennium Wheel before she told us that Alisha was not going to be an only child, and that made the day very special indeed for us! Whenever the Millennium Wheel is shown on television or in a picture, I always get a warm feeling.

Farren is now nearly four years old and, apart from being very confident, he's a real smiler. He learned to ride a two-wheel bicycle, without stabilisers, by simply jumping on one, in the playground at school, and riding it immediately. His teacher was amazed!

Most of the improvements done in the early days were done by Rob and me working eight hours a day, but Rob's next youngest brother, Geoff, also made a great contribution to the work. Although Rob and I can lay a tidy brick, plastering and bricklaying were part of Geoff's job in those days, and he was faster than we were. One morning, Geoff and I were working side by side, building a wall, and after a while I remarked that he was much faster than me. He turned on me and said, "I just hope I can work as hard as you, when I'm your age!" He said it with such force that it cheered me up no end.

However, before Rob came on the scene, James Kennedy, the vicar's son from over the road, and Paul Bird, who lived quite near, worked as weekend boys. They were in the sixth form at South Holderness School, and we still keep in touch with them. They joined in helping with all developments, and despite the fact that they were both quite brainy, would work with jobs like potting up, which can become really boring when several hundred plants are involved.

We have always been keen on the idea of making the place interesting for children, and we're still working on that one. The tower at the back was built with this in mind. However, adults have also climbed the steps and discovered that a good elevated view of the garden can be seen from this vantage point.

Evergreens had developed bit by bit and, one day, an official arrived to ask if we had planning permission. Although we had some knowledge about other aspects of the development, we honestly didn't know that permission was needed for us to sell items. However, a lifeline was extended to us with the news that if we could furnish proof that we had been in business for at least ten years, then we could automatically carry on. James's father, living over the road, had bought their Christmas tree from us ten years previously and every year after, and he was prepared to vouch for us with a letter to this effect and signed by Rev. David Kennedy!

One Sunday morning, Rob was serving a customer, a lady, when the pylon just outside our property was struck by lightning. The lady was badly affected and quite hysterical. Rob himself was shaken and the electrical charge had passed underground to the road so that (a) our alarm system was destroyed; (b) our TV in the house was ruined; and (c) two street lights across the road were put out of action! People have actually been killed by lightning, of course, but later, the pylon was removed when the wires it was supporting became obsolete.

Between our original property and the field we bought, there was a deep ditch and this was for drainage. Usually, it only contained about six inches depth of water, but after one particular bout of heavy rain, the water stood within a foot of the top. Normally, when I stood in it (in wellingtons), my head was still three or four feet below ground level.

Before we developed the land we used to have a bonfire on the field on 5th November, with twenty or thirty friends. On one such occasion, as Brenda was on her way back to the house, the cry went up, "Brenda's fallen in the ditch!" As all the party ran to help, a whole range of emotions followed, from cheerful laughter, disbelief, concern and real anxiety, as two or three helped her up the bank. She was absolutely soaked – shaken but unharmed – although she had to retire for a while to shower and find some dry clothing.

Originally, we had a small bridge across the ditch and lower down the garden the previous tenants had culverted about eighty yards of it. However, when our friends next door, who now lived in our old house, became fearful that the land on their side was slipping away, they shared the cost of having it culverted with us, and having it filled in. Built into the arrangement was that we would buy the resulting extra land from them, so that we would be able to have a bigger car park at the front.

All this took quite some time, but as a result of building work being carried out in the village, we were able to get many loads of soil delivered to help in making the area level. We were also able to lay a water pipe and an electric cable along the same area to service the garden centre further down, keeping the two supplies well apart.

In the second greenhouse we developed benches for rooting conifers with a spray system and heating wires under the cuttings. In this way, we were able to root eight thousand cuttings at a time, and we had good advice from John Read who rooted conifer cuttings on a much bigger scale. He was also kind enough to give us a full afternoon at his nursery north of York, giving us hints and advice about producing conifers, even though his spread was much bigger than ours.

Eventually, we realised that we were growing far too many conifers and that it would be much better to diversify. The rooting beds had to go, so we dismantled the greenhouse to replace it with the shop. We used some of the spare framing of the tunnel to make the support for the roof of the shop. Rob had always wanted these two to be connected and, later, he and Tristan surprised us by getting this job done while Brenda and I were on holiday. The plastic covering on the tunnel has lasted amazingly well, since that area is very sheltered from the wind.

Rob then suggested that we remove the second greenhouse and replace it with the potting shed, which has been of great use to us. These jobs took up a great deal of our time, which might have been used in other ways.

We had always wanted to have a summerhouse at the far side of the garden, so this was our next project. I rang the planning office before we started work, and was assured that planning permission was not required provided that the overall height was not more than four metres, the floor area was not more than thirty square metres and the rear of the building was at least one metre clear of the boundary. We tailored our ideas to comply with these measurements and work was started. It must be mentioned that at this point we were getting regular customers and inevitably the improvements were taking much longer to complete than when we had first started.

We wanted to have a nice tiled floor and we had these tiles stacked carefully still in their boxes. At one point, we had another call from our neighbour, Maria, that she had just seen a vehicle at the far side of her field and it appeared that our tiles were in the course of being stolen. Sadly, the car drove off so quickly that we were not able to get the car number. Had it not been for Maria's call, we would have lost the lot.

We had reached the stage of fitting the roof beams, when the building inspector arrived to tell us someone had reported that we were erecting the summerhouse without planning permission. Confidently, I assured him that we had phoned the planning authority and been told that we could go ahead provided that the parameters mentioned were not exceeded. The question then was, "Have you anything in writing?" I was completely deflated. "Surely you're not going to make us take it down", I said. He was reassuring, saying that he could see no reason why permission would not be granted, and that retrospective permission would be given if we sent in the necessary plans and forms.

Thus, instead of having the plans on the back of an envelope, I had to spend the time in doing the necessary scale drawings, enclosing the fee and submitting it all for approval. Work on the job had to be delayed until permission was given. Someone had also rung the planning authority to report that we had built the in-ground swimming pool several years previously, without permission. It began to look as if someone had a grudge against us.

We wanted to have the inside walls plastered, and although I can tackle other practical jobs, I was no good at plastering. Help came from Geoff, Rob's brother, who brought the necessary tools, gave three of us a quick lesson and then supervised and tidied up every area that we covered. However, he plastered the ceiling on his own.

We bought the two double doors second hand, and faced the front and side walls with York stone. The building has been in use ever since and in summer we have tea, coffee, soft drinks and biscuits available for customers. The small profit from this is donated to various charities, including the National Gardens Scheme (NGS). Similarly, we do garden visits for groups who book for an afternoon or evening visit with refreshments, and the profit goes to the NGS.

Just on the left of the entrance we had an enclosure with low brick walls to the rear and sides which had been used for storing sand and gravel. We knew that suitable foundations had been put in and we decided to make this the base for a wooden building to serve as a pay chalet. We always seemed to be able to get hold of wood in all shapes and sizes and eventually we had enough to get the job done.

It was Brenda, at this stage, who said, "You are going to get planning permission, aren't you?" My reply was, "You don't need planning permission for a wooden shed!" I was wrong, and this was because the garden centre is classed as industrial land. As a result, there was a further delay while the plans were drawn up, although we always had other jobs which needed doing. The shed was used as a pay chalet until about three years ago, and it is now mainly used for storing pet food, and other smaller items for sale.

It was while Paul Osman was still working with us that we found out about a large sectional shed which was available for sale over the River Humber, and Rob was keen for us to have it. They both spent two and a half days collecting the six foot sections and the roof sheets and, although it was in a reasonable state, several of the sections needed repairing. One by one, I took them into the workshop, so that rotten sections could be cut out and replaced. It was quite a while before these materials were used, but we had already decided that we would use the sections to make another shed directly alongside the long building.

We applied for planning permission and as soon as this was granted, we put in the foundations and the base. It was to be four years before any more work was done on this, but eventually we erected it and constructed a square gully to replace the guttering on the side of the long building. We have further plans for the shed, but at the present it is being used to house a static car boot sale with a range of unused items. Half the proceeds from this venture are being donated to various charities.

Paul Osman had been with us for twelve years and decided he wanted to 'fly the nest'. He had been of immense help with our development work, but a huge garden centre was opening on the outskirts of Hull, and he applied for a job there. We took some pride in the fact that, because he had worked at Evergreens for so long, he was accepted without an interview. He is still in touch with us and has now moved even further away up north, has been married to Sam for some time, and they now have little Tobias to make the family up to three and counting. Quite recently, their home was flooded with the exceptional rain and they are not likely to get back into their house for some time, so that has been really bad luck for them.

In 2007, we had the most awful floods in and around Bilton. The first we knew about this was when a customer came to the garden centre wanting bags of sand. He was followed by others, and when we realised that people were getting these to protect their homes from the floods, we were not charging, but just telling people to bring them back after the water had subsided. When we ran out of sand, people were then taking gravel in plastic bags and when this ran out, they were taking bags of topsoil. The water extended half way up our drive from the road, but we were lucky because our foundations were still well over a foot and a half above the water level.

Within four or five days, after the water had subsided, every bag which we handed out was returned to us, and in two cases with a box of chocolates as well. Sadly, many homes in the village had been swamped, and in our immediate area over a dozen families were living in static caravans parked in their drives, some for over a year.

Shortly after this, we decided to replace the up-and-over door at the back on the garage, and partition off about ten feet of our garage for use as an office. We had to apply for planning permission for this, since the room which was created would then belong to the garden centre. When we were able to go ahead, our good friend Terry, who helped with fitting out the *caravette*, rang us to say that he had some double glass doors which were going to the tip unless we wanted them. I shot round the same afternoon and they turned out to be perfect for us to install in the wall which would form the back of the office. When the space was fitted out, it provided us with a room for the office work, which previously had been dealt with in the house. In a very short time, we were wondering how we had ever managed without it.

Pandaglaze had one of their conservatories erected in the garden centre, and it was our job to greet prospective customers giving a basic introduction to the company, and then put them in touch with the secretary who would take it from there. We were paid rent for the building being in the garden centre and for quite some time, things went well. However, their sales started to diminish and, sadly, they went out of business. In exchange for the rent which was owed to us, we were able to keep the conservatory, but this left us without a contact for the product. We approached Paul Matson who supplied conservatories, to ask if he would be interested to have a similar arrangement with us. Paul and I had known each other for many years, and we now live only three doors from each other. It turned out that he was interested, and was prepared to erect a conservatory at the front of the garden centre to act as an entrance for the place.

As a result of his interest, we decided to go ahead with another extension which we had in mind, so that all the work could be co-ordinated. This development may be seen just beyond the entrance where we now have the till and Vicky's working area for floristry. Paul has a wealth of contacts for work involved with his business, and he was a tower of strength as the work progressed. The only drawback was that as a result of the land belonging to the business, the foundations had to be dug to a depth of one metre.

A selection of some of Rob's ornaments.

Work went ahead when the necessary planning permission was granted, so that within a relatively short time it was all up and running. We moved the pay area from the shed and into the new area, and Vicky then had more space to go ahead with her floristry work. For the first time, we didn't rely on DIY, but we had specialists to deal with all the main jobs. However, there were many other ways in which we were able to help with the whole project.

I doubt that any more major work will be done in the near future, but maintenance work is continuous. A good number of the paths were made well before Rob's time with us, and date back to when I was mixing concrete in a large bucket, before we had a proper mixer. Many of these and some of the low walls are in need of being replaced, and there is still work to be done on the car park. It will be quite a while before customers find us just sitting in deckchairs, and I doubt if it will ever happen.

The latest improvement which Rob and Tristan have taken in hand is the removal of many trees and bushes which have just grown too big. They have also removed the larger bushes to the left of the path beyond the old pay chalet, so that customers can see into the garden, which has been another great improvement.

Vicky, Alisha, Rob and Farren.

We could well have done without the job which turned up immediately after this. Our insurance company decided that we needed to have a fence round the pond, since it is so near the children's area. What made this seem so unreasonable, was the fact that the huge lake in East Park is fenced in only a very few places and the smaller pond where children sail their toy boats has no fencing round it whatsoever. However, we had to agree to this and the trunks of some of the larger trees cut into shorter lengths, made excellent posts for the fence. We managed to get hold of some wood for the rest fairly cheaply and so the fence was up. But the job had taken man-hours which we could well have used on other jobs. However, when it was finished we agreed that it looked quite reasonable.

Not for the first time, however, we were reminded of the saying: 'The work always expands to fill the time available.'

Rob had always been interested in making concrete castings and he has continued with this, working at home. He has now developed it into a business of his own, called 'Picta Ornaments'. Years ago, when Cynthia and Steve Myers gave up their business making garden ornaments, Rob was able to buy a number of items from them, which helped considerably in the early days. He now produces about three hundred different moulds from which he produces many hundreds of ornaments per year, as well as pavers of all shapes and sizes.

At the present time we are still working hard to diversify, so that more customers can go away with exactly what they want. Publicity is very expensive, and we know that the best sort of publicity is by 'word of mouth'. We are always pleased to see people enjoying the garden, and really pleased when children enjoy the castle and the play area.

Tailpiece: Our relationship with Rob extends over twenty-five years, and with Vicky, since before they were married, and with Alisha and Farren since they were born. Similarly, Tristan has been linked with us for fifteen years and we have known Jodie and Spencer, since before Spencer was born. Brenda and I regard them all as family, and these links have enriched our lives enormously. It is good for Brenda and me to know that when we have gone, Evergreens will carry on, but there is still much that we want to do in the meantime.

CHAPTER 12
Expeditions And Camps

In view of the fact that, over the years, I have been involved with so many expeditions and camps, I felt that this had to be dealt with in a separate chapter. I was once actually on my way to one of the Pocklington camps when I stopped at a garage to fill up with petrol. The chap who served me had been to one of our camps when he had been at school, and he never stopped talking about how much he had enjoyed it until I was driving away.

On another occasion, I had been home for four days after one of our camps, when I had a phone call from the mother of one of the boys who had been with us the previous week. After she told me who she was, she said, "He's never stopped talking about the camp since he came home, so I've just come out for half an hour to get away from him!" I'm sure that must have been a slight exaggeration, but it was good to know he had enjoyed it so much. The fact is that these are the events which youngsters remember more than anything else in their school lives.

Over the years, I have spent far more 'camping nights' involving scouting than all the school expeditions put together. Before I was married, I had clocked up the equivalent of a whole year of camping nights. (This man is a maniac!) I must admit that this includes the fourteen weeks that I spent in the army on a TA camp, and holidays under canvas with friends.

The scout summer camp was a full week. We always made the camps as economical as possible so that the cost for each boy was reasonable. In the 1940s, the fee was £1-17s-6p, and even then, I know that some of the boys were helped by skipper. And, of course, scout leaders were unpaid, then, as now.

In 1949, we went a little further afield to the Lake District. On the first night, a freak storm struck the camp at two o'clock in the morning, and every tent was blown down. Aged about sixteen, I was in a bell tent with other senior scouts, and it was fortunate that no one was struck by the main pole as it crashed to the ground. We all had to walk to the village with as much of our gear as we could find, and arrangements were made for us to use the village hall for the rest of the week. That year there were forty-eight of us in camp, and we spent a good deal of time going back to the campsite, sorting things out, and drying as much gear as we could. In spite of this, everyone enjoyed the 'camp' although a great deal of damage was done to the equipment.

I hate it when a scout leader says that he has *given up* a week of his holiday to organise a camp. I never regarded being involved with a scout activity as 'giving up' something else.

A few years later, when we were camping at Ingleton, we had to abandon camp when the river rose suddenly and flooded the site. However, this was on the last night of camp, which we spent on higher ground, in the barn.

Once, when camping in Derbyshire, a sudden gale struck the camp about halfway through the Sunday afternoon, when a coachload of parents and friends were visiting the camp. All the visitors returned to their coach and left us, leaving the empty tables which we had set up ready for a meal. Their untouched tea meal had been blown away, and spread over the countryside. My statement of, "It'll all be over in twenty minutes", was shouted by all and sundry, for some time, but by the Wednesday, no one laughed.

I was involved with the annual summer scout camp for over twenty-five years, and all the others ran without undue incident, but even the three years mentioned were enjoyed by those who took part!

One accident which happened at one of our summer camps involved two boys who were messing about with two fairly heavy metal rings fixed on the end of two ropes, and hanging from the branch of a tree, so that they were about four feet off the ground. One of the boys who was up the tree had pulled up one of the rings and, in the meantime, another boy was hanging from the other one, upside down. The one up the tree let his ring slip by accident, and it hit the other boy, John, square on the chin! This caused him to snap his mouth shut very smartly, and when he was brought to me, it was discovered he had bitten halfway through his tongue. It was as neat as could be imagined, but bleeding badly, and he was clearly in very great pain.

That year we had no vehicle in camp with us, and the nearest car was one owned by the farmer's son. He was very willing to take the boy to hospital, but unfortunately, he was one of those people who faint at the sight of blood. We had to cover John with a blanket to take him to hospital, so that the farmer's son didn't see the blood. The wound was stitched with two stitches below, two above the tongue, and one at the side, and it was as neat a piece of needlework as you could imagine.

When John and I returned to camp, the older scouts had waited up for our return. John stayed in camp for the rest of the week with mainly soft food and soup to keep him going. Two weeks later his tongue had healed completely and he was much happier!

The local authority ran a camp at Farndale in North Yorkshire, which was set up at the beginning of each summer term so that individual schools could book for a week. A bus was laid on to take a different school to the camp each Friday and the boys who had completed their week were taken back to Hull. I was involved with this from my days at East Mount, and we combined with Saltshouse School, so that sixteen pupils from there plus sixteen pupils from East Mount shared the week with two staff from each school. If all the pupils had gone from the same school it would have been difficult for the school to function with so many staff away at the same time.

For at least four years, we had the same four teachers involved and we all worked really well together. We would have a staff meeting before the camp and I would always start by saying, "I'm only coming if I can do all the cooking and catering", and the other three were quite relieved that they would be dealing with the activities in which they were more interested. I thoroughly enjoyed this aspect of any camp, since what you enjoy doing, you usually do well. The other three staff all shared the remaining jobs. We worked together extremely well, so that every camp was enjoyed whatever the weather. The fact that my cousin, Chris Brock, was one of the teachers from Saltshouse School caused slight confusion, but the pupils soon got used to it!

One year, we took over the camp from a school which will remain nameless, but every single utensil in the kitchen was dirty. We gathered the boys together and explained the situation, and mentioned also that usually when camping, all the tents had to be pitched and the camp set up, but here, all this was in place. They were great, and we all set to work washing every item which was involved in food preparation.

I was always pleased with how the boys from the two schools were on good terms with each other almost immediately, but I suppose the fact that we, as the staff also worked well together, must have 'washed off' on them. There was one camp when just sixteen pupils were all from East Mount with only Charles Smith and me as leaders, and as it happened to be the very last week of term before they were leaving the school for good, they were all in good spirits. On the second evening when we were sitting round informally having supper, one of the boys said to me, "I'm not going to call you Sir this week, I'm going to call you, Skip." In a scout troop, the leader is often known as Skipper, or Skip. I was quite pleased about him saying this, since it showed a more informal relationship. However, it never really 'caught on' because for four years my title had been more formal.

In the summer when I moved from East Mount to Dulverton it was these two schools that were at Farndale together. East Mount was a high school at that time, whereas Dulverton was a junior school with the pupils being only about eleven years old. For the week at Farndale, the East Mount boys were all around fifteen years old. In that year, East Mount and Dulverton each had sixteen pupils at Farndale with a difference of about four years between their ages. I really wondered whether relationships between the boys would be as integrated as before, but I need not have worried. The older boys from East Mount were absolutely great with the younger ones, who in turn responded really well to their friendship.

In most schools there were always a few pupils in each year group who would be described as 'difficult to handle'. The local inspector, who was responsible for the Farndale camps, always told us not to indulge in 'social experiments' when selecting pupils for the Farndale camp. By this, he meant he did not want to find that any pupil had given problems with the local residents. When we organised our own camps we made our own decisions, so when there were too many pupils who wanted to go, I put all the names in a hat and drew out the necessary numbers.

The first time I did that, two of the boys who were really pleasant lads failed to qualify, and one who did was one of the 'nuisances'. After that, I decided this was just not fair and devised the idea of sending the list of potential campers round to each member of staff in turn. Anyone who received more than three black marks was automatically barred from attending the camp, and I considered that this was a much fairer way of dealing with the problem.

When I was at East Mount School, a party of pupils and staff went every Easter holiday on a five-day youth hostelling excursion to the Lake District, and we were usually centred near Lake Windermere. A programme of walks was fixed before the event which included climbing Hellvelyn via Striding Edge. Mr Hankinson, the headmaster, led the way, and despite his age he was really fit and set up a smart pace. My function was to bring up the rear with those who were not quite such good walkers. Whether this job was allocated to me because of my powers of persuasion or because perhaps I was not as fit as the rest, I was never sure. When those in front stopped for a break, everyone else caught up and it seemed to me that they were all ready to be on their way far too soon after we at the back caught up.

East Mount staff on top of Hellvelyn.

We took the youth hostel breakfast and the evening meal plus the 'pack up' provided. When I moved on to Dulverton we established the same routine, except that each day we prepared our own midday meal and sometimes we made our own evening meal as well. I was very impressed with the way that the whole party, boys and girls, tackled all the challenges thrown at them, and in a good spirit as well.

At Neasden JH School, we continued with this expedition, and it was during this time that we experienced two extremes of weather. On one Easter expedition, it was so hot that we all sweated profusely, and as we were coming down from the top, we were passed by one man going up, who was wearing just boots, shorts and a small rucksack. This really cut across what we had told them beforehand about always wearing adequate clothing.

On another occasion, the snow was so deep that although we began to climb Hellvelyn, we had to turn back when the snow almost came up to our waists. It was the only time over many years when we didn't make the top.

I always tried to bring along emergency items which might be needed, and on one occasion, when we were at the top, I was able to produce a hammer when one boy had a nail sticking up in his boot. It was quite a while before I lived that one down. On another occasion, despite the fact that we only stayed at the top for about twenty minutes, one of the party took a photograph of me lying on my back still wearing my rucksack, but sound asleep.

Another tradition they had at Neasden JH School was always having a three-day excursion to London during the spring half term and I was pleased to continue with this. For most of the pupils it was their first visit to the capital so we tried to include as many of the landmarks in central London as possible. On one occasion, we contacted our MP (now Lord Prescott), and he was able to arrange a group visit to the Houses of Parliament. He was good enough to meet us and escort the party round. He also arranged for us to meet together privately with him to ask any questions regarding the duties of an MP. He and his wife always attended out-of-school activities, and never expected special treatment other than the usual courtesy given to visitors and parents.

Each year we had booked seats at two of the shows running in London, and in this way we were able to see many of the top rate shows which were running at the time. The choice for one evening was *Dad's Army* the stage version, or something more serious, and Mrs Ross was very indignant that I chose to go with the party to see *Dad's Army* rather than the other one. My only excuse was that I had lived through the war and had seen some of the real exploits of the Home Guard which happened at Market Weighton.

We were always able to get reasonable rates in quite good hotels because we avoided going during the summer months and on two or three occasions we were able to use Baden-Powell House which is very central and of a good standard.

Raywell Park was the Headquarters of the Humberside County Scouts and it was made available for schools to book the indoor accommodation for a full week during the summer term. My own involvement started during my time at Dulverton JH School and continued after I had moved to Neasden JH School. The accommodation provided two- and four-bedded rooms to sleep twenty-four, a kitchen, dining room, meeting room and four smaller rooms. There were six acres of land for outdoor activities with some woodland but mainly grass, and an orchard with a number of cabins, one of which could be used for extra accommodation if required.

We would book the place for five days in the summer term; the girls went from Monday to Wednesday and the boys from Wednesday to Friday, so Wednesday was the change-over day. One of the mothers, who was an excellent caterer, went along for three days and worked in the kitchen while the girls were there, and I covered the meals for the second half of the week. Various activities took place for each group, including a hike to Skidby to see the mill and the village itself. The Humber Bridge was being constructed over the period of these visits, and we were able to let each group see the progress which was being made.

The school camps at Pocklington started for me when I moved to Dulverton and were carried on with Neasden when I moved there. Mr Dale – the head at Dulverton – had used the site many times before as the farmer was an old friend of his. There was a small stream and, apart from the fun of this, I always liked to be sure that all campers had a really good wash every morning. More than once I had heard of a pupil returning home after such an expedition and the mother had found his soap was unused and still in its wrapper. This never happened with us. The camps were for the third-year boys and we usually had twenty-five pupils during the first week of the summer holidays. We had some of the girls asking why they couldn't come but in the end only six of the girls came, so after that, we decided to keep it for boys only. The five best campers were able to go the following year as 'tent group leaders', and this worked really well.

The pupils going to the Pocklington camp had the use of all the camping equipment which Mr Dale had accumulated over the years, and I made a large tent – a marquee, really – which would accommodate all the campers sitting at tables for meals. If there was some cash left over at the end of a camp, it was shared between all those who had attended. However, I decided that as they were having the use of all the camping gear, this money would be used to buy some new item of equipment or replace something which was worn out. In this way, we were able to improve the equipment slightly year on year.

One year, when we were camping at Pocklington, the farmer's son from the nearby farm, who was about the same age as our pupils, made friends with some of our boys. The first that I really knew about this was when one day he was having the midday meal with us. That evening, he brought his gear along, moved into one of the tents and stayed with us for the rest of the week. On our last day, his father came to thank us for having him and brought a huge bag of potatoes for the boys to share and take home with them. He also said that if we ever wanted a change of campsite, he had a field nearer to the town which we could use.

This was perfect timing, because where we were, the farmer was not getting any younger and he always worried about the possibility of the top gate being left open, so that his cows would escape. This never happened, but he still worried about it. His wife worried about the boys crossing the road to fetch water from the farm. This offer solved the problem and was also brilliant news, because it turned out that the new site had a much bigger stream which subsequent campers really enjoyed damming, and the source of fresh water was nearer. We were able to use this site for several more years before I retired. Just upstream from the campsite, a smaller shallower stream joined the larger one and the resulting deeper water was really warm, so this became known as 'the tropics'.

All of us went to the cinema in Pocklington on the first evening, so that when we returned to camp everyone was quite tired and the boys settled to sleep rather better. We also had one day on the beach north of Bridlington, and we visited the indoor pool in Pocklington at least once. One year, the boys made a coracle, a raft and a simple canoe, and we went to the head of Market Weighton Canal to try them out. They all floated, and carried passengers, but quite a few of the campers fell into the water. It was a warm afternoon and some of that may have been deliberate!

On the last evening, we always had a campfire singsong and at the end we had various presentations. This was definitely a 'fun' thing and each pupil received a chocolate bar or a bag of sweets. Prizes were awarded for the best suntan, the hardest worker, the one who grumbled the least, the best potato peeler and so on. Most of the citations were very much 'tongue in cheek'.

Having the minibus augmented by parents' and staff cars made it very much easier for us when sports teams were playing away. In the summer term, we had one-day excursions, which were really a carry-over from the time when most children had fewer summer holidays and some had none at all.

When I had been at Fountain Road Boys School, the entire school all went off on the same day, along with very many parents. I seem to remember that there were as many as eight coaches lined up outside the school on excursion day. Towards the end of my schooldays, they were termed 'educational visits' and the teachers in each year group decided where and when they would go. I didn't really mind where they went, as long as they all enjoyed it, in the more informal atmosphere which usually prevailed. One year, I was rather disappointed with a group who were taken to Whitby. They were dropped off for some free time, and I was dismayed to see the entire party go straight into Woolworths! We tried to dissuade the parents from letting them bring much money with them, but by the time aunties and uncles had 'dibbed in', all the pupils were very well financed.

The Wembley day trip was a yearly event, and normally a train was booked for a whole group of schools. One year, the rugby final at Wembley involved Hull FC versus Hull Kingston Rovers, and on that occasion we went by coach. Naturally, there was a great deal of local interest and some wag had put up a notice at the far end of Clive Sullivan Way, just outside Hull, which read, 'Last one to leave, put the lights out!'

The ladies in the school kitchen caused some amusement for the pupils, because only one of them was wearing the black and white scarf of Hull FC, whereas all the rest wore the red and white scarf of Kingston Rovers. This caused a great deal of good natured banter!

Tailpiece: We were very lucky that so many of the staff were prepared to be involved, so that all these visits could take place. With all the present rules regarding health and safety, I understand that teachers are more cautious about running out-of-school activities, which is a great shame. I always thought that this was part of the job and, naturally, scout leaders and other voluntary youth leaders regarded such activities as definitely part of their job.

CHAPTER 13
Chris And His Travels

The front bedroom in our bungalow has always been known as 'Chris's Room'. This is largely because, in spite of his travels, he has always returned at regular intervals, and the complete story of his life would form a book in itself. When he was about eighteen, he visited Israel on two occasions and worked in a Kibbutz, despite the fact that he is not Jewish! On the second visit, he met Carol and for a while they were living in the London area, where we visited them from time to time.

At one point they moved from one area to another, and I went down with my van to help with this. When I arrived, they were at work, and so I started moving their belongings into the van to save time. Much of the stuff was in the hall and along one side of the staircase, and as I was moving it all into the van, it occurred to me that some neighbour might very well come and challenge me, or even report the situation to the police. No one noticed. I could have been a burglar and not a soul even knew I was there!

One of our visits coincided with our wedding anniversary, and it was Carol who arranged the celebration meal for us at a restaurant in North London. Both Chris and Carol had what might be described as 'wanderlust', and I feel sure that Chris could write a really excellent book about all his travels.

During their time in London, they bought a VW campervan which stayed at Evergreens, although they came back at weekends, staying with us and working on it. Many improvements were made and they planned to cross the Sahara Desert in it, like you do! In fact, this would be an enormous project and not to be taken lightly, if at all. Just before they set off, it was discovered a new engine was needed for their campervan, and our good friend, John Wells, who had a garage just across the road from us, loaned Chris a car to go over to the West Riding to collect a reconditioned engine, which John then fitted for him. Brenda and I were invited to go down through France with them for the four of us to have a holiday together on the south coast near Bordeaux. They would then travel on to North Africa and we would travel north back home.

As it happened, Brenda was looking after her mother and sister at that time, but she didn't want to spoil it for me, so I went with them in their van, and returned by rail at the end of the fortnight. Allowing for all the school excursions, camps, visits and so on, you will have gathered that Brenda is a wife in a million, but I knew that, even before we were married.

The three of us had a marvellous fortnight in the middle of September. And every day the sun shone from morning until night. We then drove to Bordeaux, where I left them, feeling rather sad, knowing that I would not be seeing them for a very long time, and aware that the journey they were contemplating was very hazardous indeed.

My own journey back home was by train and that was a nightmare. The train to Paris was absolutely crowded, and by the time I arrived home, I felt really shattered!

Chris and Carol travelled south and went on the short journey across the western end of the Mediterranean Sea to Morocco. At this point, a local mechanic informed them that the filter in their engine was completely useless for the journey they were about to attempt. Using bits and pieces from an old washing machine, he fashioned another filter from scratch, which would give their engine the necessary protection from the dust and sand which they were likely to encounter.

They travelled south across the desert and there was at least one occasion when they could easily have lost their lives. The roads are very basic, and at one point they decided to take a short cut on a road which was seldom used, but would cut two or three hundred miles off the journey. After going down this track for over a hundred miles, they saw that the road ahead was completely covered by the effect of a sandstorm. They had to make the decision whether to turn back, or take a run at it and try to get through.

They chose the second option and found themselves stranded right in the middle. Attempts were made to dig the wheels out, but this effort was all in vain, and they finally gave up and sat in the van feeling very, very depressed. They had heard stories of people who had died under similar circumstances, and they really thought that this was going to happen to them!

The hours passed, when suddenly they saw some movement on the horizon. Within a few minutes, three large army lorries pulled up, and the officer in charge started to berate the pair of them for leaving the main track. Apparently a family of six people had all been found dead in their vehicle under similar circumstances, only six weeks before! The vehicles were a desert patrol and the chance of anyone coming regularly along the same track was very unlikely indeed. They both stood there meekly, knowing that when the abuse subsided, they would be pulled through the drift by one of the heavy army vehicles.

Finally, they reached Nigeria where they were delayed for a few days, until they were able to secure clearance to travel east, and after more delays and problems, they ended up in Mombasa. Here they contacted us, and Carol's parents as well, with the news that they were safe. Amazingly, at this point, Carol met a man from the same village where her parents lived, in England, and what was even more amazing was that he was returning to the UK by air on the following day. He took a letter which she had been intending to post, and passed it on to her parents personally!

Chris and Brenda in Australia.

Brenda and I had no idea of their future plans, but they sold the van and flew to Australia, where they planned to stay for a year. Six months or so later, we flew out to see them and stayed for three weeks. This was the point when Dave came into the story again, because he had also flown over to Australia with his cousin and they planned to stay for about six months. Dave is another one whose movements are always unpredictable and I believe that we only found out about this very shortly before we were meeting him again, but in Australia. Up to that point, David's main claim to fame was his ability at boxing. He was a member of the St. Paul's Boxing Club in Hull, and at the age of fifteen he was the National Boxing Champion of all England at his age and weight.

When Brenda and I landed in Sydney, Chris was working and so it was Carol who met us. She told us that they were both lodging thirty miles inland from Sydney, with Greg, one of the sons of Bert and Sheila Shipton, who we would get to know very well indeed. She explained that if we had been based with them, we would have wasted a great deal of time getting to and from Sydney each day. Unfortunately, Chris and Carol had not been able to get time off work for the first two weeks of our stay.

However, they had booked us into a self-catering apartment right on the front at Bondi Beach, and they provided us with a huge bag of provisions to start us off. Now Brenda has a very fair skin and when we went out to the nearest chemist for some sun tan cream, the lady behind the counter was very concerned for her. There were warnings about staying out of the sun, AT ALL TIMES, and she recommended the highest numbered cream that it was possible to obtain. The beach at Bondi is divided into two areas – one for surfboarders, and one for swimmers and bathers. This works very well, since everyone appeared to obey the rules.

Chris and Carol were with us every day after work, so we would have the evenings together, plus weekends. They each had a car and both arrived to be with us every weekday at about five o'clock and often earlier. For our first weekend they had hired a yacht and the party included Dave and his cousin who had also arrived in Australia by then. We enjoyed a great weekend with them all, and in the second week, Chris loaned us his car so we could explore over a wider area. On the second weekend, we all went down to Callala, about forty miles south of Sydney where Bert and Sheila had a beach-side house which they used for holidays.

On that weekend, there were eight of us in the party, including Dave and his cousin, and the weather was perfect for the whole time. After Sunday evening, there were just four of us left for the last week – Chris and Carol plus Brenda and me. On the Monday evening all the maps, photographs and other information were brought out and we heard all about their problems crossing the Sahara. The extreme danger involving the trip was illustrated time and again, and we were relieved that we found this out *after* the adventure was over, rather than earlier!

The seminar continued on the Tuesday evening, and was only finished after another hour or so on the Wednesday evening! We would not have wanted to miss those three evenings for anything. On our last Wednesday, Carol was notified that she was needed at her workplace, and Chris was not well pleased. However, those two days were spent mostly on the beach or in the sea.

After we left Callala on the Friday, we had been invited to a barbeque with Bert and Sheila at Rooty Hill where Carol re-joined us. We had a great evening with all the family and Bert spent some time showing me his workshop and giving me a complete tour of the grounds. They were obviously really happy at Rooty Hill, and it must have been a real wrench when the land was taken over by compulsory purchase, but they chose to live permanently at Callala. We then went on to Chris and Carol's place for the night, and Chris took us to the airport the next day to catch a plane en route for home. Yet again, it had been a really memorable time for us!

Shortly after we had left, Chris and Carol took several months to travel all around Australia along with Dave. It should be recorded that Dave has a tremendous ability to fall asleep if the conversation lapses. When telling the story later on, Chris remarked cheerfully that they only woke him up if there was something interesting to see. Having been good friends from their time at school they can say what they like to each other without either taking offence!

When Chris and Carol returned to England, they came to stay with us for a year while Chris completed a joinery course in Hull. However, at that time, Brenda's mother and sister were both living with us, and our friend Nick Matson was staying with us as well. So we bought a static caravan for Chris and Carol to live in, and this was placed in the drive. We arranged for mains electricity and water, and connected the toilet up to the main sewer. Carol scraped off all the old wallpaper in the van and improved the interior in many other ways, so they had their own place but were able to use other facilities in the house.

Chris was always a great one for springing surprises on us, so after the year was over, they bought a yacht – *Wild Rose* – which was based at Walton-on-the-

Naze. They moved back to London, where they were both able to get a better job than in Hull. For about two years, they worked on the boat, staying aboard at weekends, and I went down several times to help with the work. One weekend, Rob and his friend, Wayne, came down with me and we all had a mini-cruise.

My contribution to the improvements on the yacht was to make a full set of cushions and mattresses with piped edges. (I have an ancient sewing machine, over a hundred years old, which still works perfectly!) Over the years, I had acquired some skill in using it, as mentioned earlier, when I actually made a small marquee tent.

Chris on his yacht.

Originally, the intention was for them to sail right round the world, and in 1994 Brenda and I went to see them off, but sadly things didn't work out and they returned to England. They set off a second time, and again we went to see them off, but the atmosphere was a little tense. I think that as a result of working so hard on the yacht, they had rather lost touch with each other, and before we visited Chris when he reached Tenerife, Carol had left. The arrangement was that Chris would have the boat for three years, and Carol would have it for a further three years, and they would each do their 'own thing'. Brenda and I were really sorry that they separated, since Carol had always accepted us as 'family', and the four of us had enjoyed many good times together.

Chris made preparations to sail across the Atlantic Ocean to the Caribbean, on his own, and I asked him casually how long he imagined it would take him to complete the crossing. He knew very well the hidden reason for me wanting to know and so, smiling, he said, "Some people have done it in a fortnight. I might be as long as three weeks, but don't ring the coastguard until a month has elapsed!" Twenty-two days later he rang us to say he had made it. He had taken part in a race to cover the crossing and achieved a plaque which he displayed in the yacht. When he arrived, it seemed there were several days of partying which were thoroughly enjoyed by all the contestants. He was in no great hurry and he stayed on St. Marten for a few months working on a building which had suffered damage from a hurricane. During that time, one of his sisters, Sherrie, stayed with him for six weeks, cruising around, and Brenda and I stayed for a fortnight of that time. We sailed round Richard Branson's island, in the British Virgin Islands, but no invitation was received for us to stay with him! All around us there were yachts much bigger than the one we was sharing, so we were definitely the 'poor relations', but as we mixed with the others ashore, we seemed to fit in quite well.

When we had left, Chris set off again to sail through the Panama Canal. He told us quite happily that sailing across the Pacific Ocean is even more hazardous than crossing the Atlantic Ocean, which we would rather have not known, and it was two months later before we heard from him again. He rang from the Galapagos Islands in great spirits and he was obviously enjoying himself. During the remainder of the journey, he actually spent twenty-two consecutive days without seeing ANYTHING on the horizon at all!

He arrived in New Zealand in late 1997, and Brenda and I were there to meet him. Before he landed, he had run out of fuel and was becalmed for a few days. By then we were staying with my cousin John and his wife Sue, in Hawkes Bay. We had flown from England with John's mother, my Aunty Joan, who was staying for six months. By that time, she was 'getting on' and needed a wheelchair when travelling. This was quite an experience for us because, as she had special service, we went with her and we were always the first to get on the plane!

When we landed there were two cars to meet us, John and his good neighbour, so again we had five star service. When Chris landed in the Bay of

Islands a week later, he hired a car and came over to where we were staying. His first words were, "What a marvellous country. I could live here!" We were expecting him to look a bit weather-beaten, but in fact we had never seen him looking so fit! During the entire crossing he had obviously looked after his health, and he had even made his own bread on a quite regular basis. We met up again with Greg, who by then, amazingly, had relocated to New Zealand, and was living close by with his family. We were able to visit him, his wife Catherine and their children, Sarah and Philip, and we even had a weekend break with them, when later, they were all living in northern New Zealand.

Brenda and I toured North Island with Chris for a fortnight, and worked our way back to the yacht in the Bay of Islands. We had hoped to have a little cruise, but the weather was not too good and the sea was choppy, so we just spent time together. At the end of the week, we flew back to England with more happy memories of our relationship with Chris. By this time, Carol had moved on and no longer wanted the yacht, so they sold it, severing their link completely.

The following year Chris returned to Evergreens and found out that a huge yacht, to be called *Boadicea*, was being built in a shipyard in Holland. He was able to join the crew as a deckhand joiner, and the yacht was launched, with a twenty-four man crew. It also had a guest area which could accommodate twelve people in great comfort. In a relatively short time, Chris was promoted to Chief Deckhand. When the yacht visited England later, it was berthed near Tower Bridge in London, and all the crew were able to have two visitors on board for the Saturday afternoon and have a tour of the entire facilities. Chris invited Brenda and me for the whole weekend, and booked us into a nearby hotel.

About the middle of 2000, Chris left *Boadicea* to work on a much smaller yacht in the Mediterranean, to gain more experience, and this lasted until October 2001. Following that, he came home again for six months, travelling to different parts of the country taking various courses and exams, which would culminate with him gaining his Master's Three Thousand Ticket. This would enable him to take charge of any seagoing yacht up to three thousand gross tons, anywhere in the world. We're not thinking of rowing boats here; a ship of this size would be 100 metres long (or about 330 feet).

He then re-joined *Boadicea*, and it was round this time when Talia came into his life. She too was working on the yacht and along with her other work she always accompanied Mr Grundy on his photographic expeditions. When they returned to the boat, she would develop the slides which had been taken, and Mr Grundy would indicate which ones he wanted printing. When Talia decided to leave the yacht, Mr Grundy wanted Chris to take over the photographic work and gave them both two days, so that Talia could brief Chris regarding what was required. Talia then went back home to New Zealand.

In late 2003, Brenda and I were on holiday in France, when in a telephone conversation with me Chris said, "You'd better start saving up for a wedding present!" When I told Brenda of this, she was sure that Chris had been joking, so the following day, we rang him back. It seemed that his relationship with Talia had not only involved photography, but that they had become rather close!

Celebrating one of our wedding anniversaries.
Brenda, Freya, Talia, Chris and me.

The next news we heard was that Talia was expecting a baby, and we immediately made plans to visit New Zealand around the time the baby was due. Chris had secured leave from the yacht, and Talia was then living in Auckland where they had bought a house. We were able to meet Talia's parents and stay with them for a short time at Te Puke, where they had an ostrich farm. The rapport between us all was immediate, and it was agreed that we would be Grandma and Grandad on Chris's side. They would be Oma and Opa, since Talia's father, Ewalt (pronounced Avolt), is second generation Dutch. We then went back to Auckland, although we had to move out of the house for the birth, because Talia had settled for a water birth, and our room was needed for the pool! Talia's mother, Penny, moved in; we went off for twenty-four hours, and the little one came along right on time.

The new arrival was a little girl, and everything had gone swimmingly. (Sorry about that!)

Three or four days had passed and they still didn't have a name for the baby. On the fifth day, I said, "Look here. She'll be going to school and the teacher will ask her name, and she won't be able to answer." However, they finally decided on Freya Roseilla. Roseilla is the middle name of Freya's great-oma on her father's side of the family.

All too soon, the time came for us to fly home, but it had been THE most marvellous holiday. We were invited back for her first Christmas and we all stayed on the farm. There were eleven of us, and the family observed certain traditions, one of which was that every person should buy a Christmas present for everyone else, but that no present was to cost more than five dollars. Chris broke that rule, because he proceeded to present Talia with an engagement ring! There wasn't a dry eye in the house. Each present was unwrapped separately so that everyone could see all the items. The children did a marvellous job of collecting the wrapping paper and keeping the place tidy.

Talia's brother, Troy, and his wife, Kelly, also spent Christmas on the farm, with their three children, Jervis, Malachi and Brijana. Troy is an oarsman and is very fit, and on the last day it was quite hot and he took his shirt off. He was very impressive!

On Christmas night, another tradition was that each adult would write a poem about one of the others. Brenda was in bed early because she was not too well, and I saw Talia helping Chris with his offering. However, I did manage something on my own, even though it may not have been very good.

On Boxing Day morning, Ewald produced a fresh ostrich egg, bored two holes in it with an electric drill, and I was invited to blow it. The contents were collected in a basin and we ALL had scrambled egg for breakfast! In the afternoon loads of family arrived including Talia's grandparents, Tini and Kryjn

– great-oma and great-opa for Freya. We had met them before and even visited their home and they were lovely! Brenda and I flew back home shortly after, and Chris later flew back to the *Boadicea*.

In 2005 Chris was appointed the captain of *Boadicea*. From originally joining the crew of the yacht as deckhand joiner, in a relatively short time he had succeeded in being appointed as captain, and we felt very proud of him!

Chris and Talia's wedding.

Chris and Talia were married on 19th October 2008, in Auckland. Around that time, Brenda was having treatment from a doctor who said that it would be most unwise for her to fly on such a long journey at that time. Brenda was her usual expansive self, saying that as we had waited so long for this event, it would be a shame for us both to miss it, so I went on my own, feeling very guilty. It was helpful for them to have someone to look after Freya while they went all over, making arrangements for the wedding. I had flown to New Zealand about a fortnight before the wedding, since Vicky was due to give birth again and I really didn't want to miss that either.

The wedding was fantastic. Talia looked radiant, and I know that is a cliché, but she really did. Chris looked really smart, and Freya was lovely. After the ceremony, about fifty of us, relatives and friends, sat down to a splendid meal, followed by speeches. I was allowed to speak immediately after Ewald, which illustrated really well how much Brenda and I had been accepted as family. I regarded this as a great privilege.

The following morning I awoke to the sight of three children, Freya, Jarvis and Malachi, standing round my bed all pointing their toy guns in my direction. They were the only ones who were up! Chris and Talia had spent the night in a hotel, and I was the only one available to give the children their breakfast. Needless to say, I rose to the occasion.

Talia's mum, Penny, had organised a huge picnic for the following day, so several car-loads of us went along to the north of Auckland where Chris and Talia had purchased three acres of land. Chris showed me the site where their house was to be built, and gave me details of exactly how it was going to look. On the journey there and back, Jarvis, who had just learnt to read, entertained us with extracts from his joke book.

However, the very next day I was set to fly back home, with fingers crossed that I would make it in time before Farren was born. In the event, Farren was a bit late, but everything passed off really well. Rob and Vicky had no idea at the time whether they were going to have another girl or a boy until the actual birth. All they hoped was that everything would go well, and it did! Farren's middle name is also 'Whitehouse', the same as Rob, to perpetuate his great grandad, and Alisha's middle name is 'May', to keep her nana's name in the family.

During his time on *Boadicea*, Chris had established a very good relationship both with Mr Grundy and his wife, so that when they came to sell the yacht in 2009, in spite of it being the end of an era, Mr Grundy invited Chris to advise him regarding the purchase of a much smaller boat. This is to be used around Bermuda, where they have a house, so that Mr Grundy could continue his interest in wildlife photography. Later, when he was having his eighty-fifth birthday celebrations, he invited both Chris and Talia over to Australia for a fortnight, all expenses paid! By then Freya was growing up fast, and so she spent a week of this time staying with Chris's sister, Sherrie, and her husband Bryn. She spent the second week with Brenda and me, and this made us feel like real grandparents!

Chris on *Talisman C*, of which he is the captain.

Towards the end of 2009, Chris secured another job in Turkey, in charge of the construction team building a new yacht, *Talisman C*, which was completed in 2011. Chris was even allowed to launch the yacht, and we have the photographs to prove it! Following the launch, Chris took over as captain and after a few 'teething troubles', they spent the winter touring in the Caribbean. The owner has two brothers, and all three of them are married with families, and each family has time allocated to use the yacht.

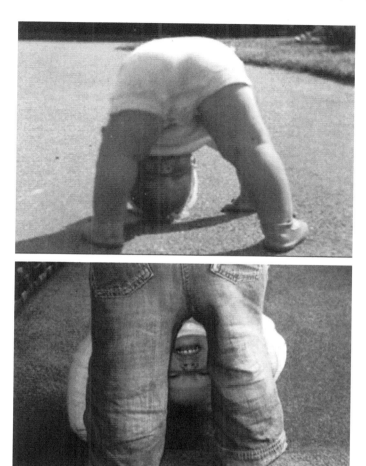

Me at 11 months, 1933 (top) – Freya at about 3 years old, 2005.

In the meantime, Chris and Talia have had a house built at Addingham, near Leeds, so that Talia can spend time at Leeds University on an art course, and Freya can attend the Montessori School which is quite close for them. Brenda and I have seen the house at various stages during its construction, and Chris was quite surprised by Brenda's ability at scaling to each floor, before the proper staircases had been fitted! No expense has been spared either with the fittings or the furnishings. They were very lucky indeed with their choice of builder, because all their requirements were met and the house was completed on time. Eventually, they will go back to New Zealand, and Brenda and I are just hoping that we shall live long enough to have one more visit there to see the house that Chris will be building.

Brenda, Talia, Freya and Chris at Evergreens.
Freya made her own wreath for the front door.

Tailpiece: In our lives, Brenda and I have been very lucky indeed to have had so much contact with young people. From time to time, we hear in the news of old people (and eighty IS old, even today) being lonely and being on their own. Neither of us can imagine what life would be like without having so much contact with young people and families and friends. It's nice for us to have holidays and get away from the normal routine at home, but we always look forward to coming back, as much as the start of any holiday.

CHAPTER 14
Reminiscing And Looking To The Future

You will, no doubt, have gathered that Brenda and I have enjoyed a long and happy life. We've had our share of sadness, which is inevitable, but as far as our health is concerned, we have reason to be thankful. Years ago, Brenda was diagnosed with breast cancer, but it was located in good time, and as a result of an operation being carried out very promptly, it was not as serious as it might have been. Following therapy, which involved me drawing all over her with a marker pen, when the original guidelines started to fade, she recovered well, and there has been no sign of any recurrence.

I have had two hernia operations which were both successful, as were the two cataract operations – one on each eye. The more serious problem was a detached retina, but as a result of very prompt action, that operation was also a total success.

The moral here is: Don't ask anyone over the age of sixty how they are, because many of them will take the question literally and reply in great detail. Rather than that, just say, "You look really well", although even that is risky!

Brenda and I were both turned thirty when we married. We were hoping that we would have a family, and there was just one time when we thought we had 'made it', but it was not to be.

Brenda has short-term memory loss, but we both still enjoy life, largely because we have a wide circle of friends. Ron Lawson and I have known each other since we were both eleven, and at the end of a good evening out, he will often say, "Well, if we don't wake up in the morning, we've had a good night tonight."

This remark is not said in a serious way, but indicates that we've had a drink or two, and it is almost always followed by a punch on my upper arm. I well remember my stag night, when he sat next to me all evening, and the following morning my arm was black and blue. His other saying, in the last ten years, has been to indicate that we're both living on borrowed time, and that our normal life expectancy is three score years and ten.

When Ron married Jill (she's much younger than him), I was asked to be Ron's best man and this was so long ago, they are now grandparents many times over. They have a son and a daughter, who between them have produced eight grandchildren for Jill and Ron. I am godfather to Ian, who lives in the Midlands and Jane lives in the family home in Saltshouse Road.

Eighty-one years old is as good a time as any to take stock of the situation, and we realise that however long we live, most of our life is over. The question arises, "What are we going to do now?"

We have spent the last twenty-five years building up the garden centre and the gardens, with a great deal of help, and there are still many improvements that we want to add. Rob has a much more practical attitude to this. His main aim is to make the gardens easier to look after. But we all want to make them more attractive, so that customers will enjoy looking round. We are really pleased when people do this, and even happier when children enjoy playing here.

In addition, Brenda and I want to fit in some extra holidays, before we are too old to travel.

Meantime, we know that we're not going to last forever, and we take great comfort in the fact that our 'affairs' are all in order. We're pleased that our good friends, John Horth and John Clarke, have agreed to be our executors. John Clarke and his wife Jenny have spent a good part of their lives in the Far East, and if they had stayed in the UK we would have seen a GREAT deal more of each other. However, John has assured me that if anything happens to us of a 'final farewell' nature, he will be on the next plane back to the UK. We have been real friends with John Horth and his wife Jean, for over thirty years. When their offspring, Lynn and Steve, were younger, we had many holidays with them, in France, and we are still great friends.

Brenda and I are both linked with Portobello Methodist Church and the scout group is also linked there, but a good many years ago, the Church was much stricter than it is now. One minister we had, just after the war, took great pleasure in telling everyone that at his wedding, the toast was drunk in water! The same man asked questions regarding a 'lucky dip' which the scouts were having at a fayre which was being organised. The question was whether all the items in the lucky dip be worth the shilling which was being charged to have a go.

The answer, of course was that some would be about the same, but some would be worth a bit more, and some a bit less. The minister banned it immediately, because he regarded it as gambling. What he would think of the national lottery today would never be open to question.

I have been known to rescue a spider in the shower and carry it, in cupped hands, to a place of safety. And yet, there I was in the infantry where I was a drill and weapon training instructor. I suppose that if I ever had the misfortune to be in the front line in a war, the idea of 'kill or be killed' would prevail.

I can become emotional to an embarrassing degree, if cruelty to children is involved. Although I can deal well with cuts and scratches, I really don't know how I would fare if faced with a really gruesome accident, where blood, real pain and disfigurement was involved.

Me in my workshop.

When you start looking back on your life, all sorts of incidents come to mind. As I was writing this, it occurred to me for the first time, how disappointed my mother must have been when I stopped learning to play the piano. Both my parents were musical, and my mother was a really talented pianist. If a piece of music was placed in front of her, she could play it on the piano as if she was reading a chapter in a library book!

She started me with lessons immediately after we went to Market Weighton and I stuck it for about three years. Then, I realised I did not have the aptitude, and gave up. Before the war, my father had been in a dance band, the Paramount Players, and he played the saxophone and was the vocalist. On reflection, they must have both been disappointed with me, as far as musical ability is concerned. My only talent in this area is being able to sing 'patter' songs quite loudly and in tune. My rendering of, 'Jonathan, Joseph, Jeremiah, etc.', is a legend!

When I was much younger, I was rather shy in coming forward. When we first went to Market Weighton, William, the eldest son of the family, would take me all over the place visiting customers, which I really enjoyed. One journey involved a visit to a huge chicken farm where I wandered about as he spoke to the owner. After a short time, I heard the sound of a car being started, and thinking that William had forgotten about me, I started to run back to the house. A large group of chickens also started to panic, and before I knew what was happening, about a dozen had flown over the wire and out of the pen. Of course, William must have thought I was chasing them, and on the journey home, no word was spoken. Why I didn't just tell him what had really happened, I shall never know, but that was the end of my outings with him.

Later, when I was a teenager, my father decided I was not getting enough exercise and insisted that we both went for a walk together. I really, really didn't want to go, but he insisted, so we went. Over the entire walk, which involved about three miles, not a word was spoken, and when we arrived home, my uppermost thought was, "What the dickens was that all about?" Only recently have I thought that he might have wanted us to have a conversation together, and didn't really know how to start.

Until about ten years ago, I was carrying my age very well, and when someone new to me found out how old I was, they were genuinely surprised, and in a good way. Within the last five years, I must have aged. On one occasion, a lady actually offered me her seat! In a queue at an airport, one of the officials motioned to us to leave the queue and pushed us to a desk which was obviously intended for privileged passengers. We quite enjoyed that experience! What really rankles is when someone speaks in a condescending way as if to indicate 'poor old thing'. In a similar way, it is quite dreadful when anyone talks to someone in a wheelchair in a sympathetic or pitying way.

The garden at Evergreens, taken from our bedroom window.

Over the years, we've had a great deal of help from a number of friends. When Brenda's mum and Betty were living with us, we had a team of eight carers, who worked on a rota. As a result of this help, Brenda was able to have some relief, so that we could have time to ourselves, and the odd holiday. Heading this team was Margaret Gibson, who lives just up the village and, over the years, she has been a tower of strength for us.

Shirley Stathers had been coming to us once a week from the time when Brenda was still at the bank, and over many years her help was invaluable. In addition, if I was stuck for one or two of the clues in the so-called 'quick crossword' in the morning paper, she could always come up with the answers!

More recently, Coral McGowan, who goes to bingo with Margaret, has been helping Brenda for two hours on four days every week. Coral started coming just before the time, around a year ago, when Brenda had some health problems.

Eventually, Brenda had to go into hospital for ten days, and she lost the use of her legs. Without going into too much detail, Coral's help was invaluable, and in a relatively short time Brenda recovered really well and was walking as well as ever.

Later, Brenda decided that she would stop driving her car. I was disappointed by this because I thought that she drove really well. She always went to Hornsea every Saturday morning and met friends at the cafe which overlooks the sea. When Brenda sold her car, Coral immediately offered to take her to Hornsea every week in her own car, so that Coral has also made friends with the 'Saturday morning group'.

"Regrets, I've had a few, but then again too few to mention . . ." and the lyrics end with the words, "I did it my way". I suppose we all have regrets about some of the things which have happened in our lives, and it isn't good enough just to say 'I did it my way'.

But what else can we say?

There can't be many couples who have never had children of their own, but who nevertheless have four 'grandchildren'. I have already written about how delighted we were, after Alisha was born, that Farren came along five years later. Chris and Talia, too, were really pleased that even before Freya was born, she would be our 'granddaughter'. Finally, when Jodie and Tristan produced Spencer, they too (along with Tristan's mum, Esme) were pleased that I would be 'grandad', with Brenda as an extra grandma. And we love them all.

An old lady aged ninety-three lived near us when I was a boy, whose first words every morning when she woke up were, "Oh God, am I still here?" I always through that was REALLY sad. Brenda and I both have our faith and we know that in the end, we shall die, but we still have things we want to do. However, it would be great if we could reach the stage that we have done everything in life we want to do, and we're ready to go.

But we haven't reached that stage yet!